HOW TO SUCCEED ON PURPOSE

Modern Wisdom & Inspirational Truth
for Succeeding
Each Day of Your Life

TW Hawk

~ Light Reads ~
Big Sur • Amsterdam • New York

HOW TO SUCCEED ON PURPOSE:
Modern Wisdom & Inspirational Truth
for Succeeding Each Day of Your Life

Back cover author photo by Michelle Magdalena.

Printed in the United States of America.

ISBN: 978-1-7323052-4-3

Light Reads Publishing
PO Box 123
Big Sur, CA 93920

For more principals, meditations, video and audio content visit
www.TruthOnPurpose.com

For Sage and Sol,
my favorite souls.

For Harmony and Hudson,
my greatest loves.

For Heather and Sidney,
lifesavers.

For Big Sur,
with epic gratitude for your
inspiration and healing,
magnificent beauty,
ineffable magic.

For like-minded spirits,
weavers of love,
harbingers of joy,
who further the inclination of light.

CONTENTS

SUCCESS

SPIRIT

CONFLICT & COMMUNICATION

PROBLEMS & SOLUTIONS

HEART-CENTERED LIVING

ACTION

CHILD'S PLAY

MATTER

GARDEN-VARIETY INSPIRATION

ALMOST HOME

*We are wisps of consciousness
having an ephemeral experience.*

~ Truth

INTRODUCTION

It all came to a head in a single month at the end of a year. To succinctly describe the crisis: check the boxes for health, career, finances, relationship, domicile and then light them all on fire. "This is not working for me" became the categorical response to what had once been an extraordinary life. Even my body had vetoed the status quo.

As it all came crashing down, I had a profound sense everything was happening for a reason. The pile-up of challenges, included minor surgery, was propelling me toward something. Something new. Something different. Marilyn Monroe once said: "Sometimes things fall apart so they can fall together better."

I found myself divinely guided to the very things I had been seeking: adventure, inspiration, community, healing, nature, spirit, love, support, being seen... The call of these prospects was located somewhere new. It wasn't on the other side of the world, but it was a world away from the life I knew. And it meant re-locating.

My path became clear. "Determined to save the only life I could save," as Mary Oliver poeticized, I took the plunge: I chose to live. To thrive. To follow joy and purpose. To step into Truth. To become the artist I longed to be while I'd handled the careers of so many other artists for so long. I stepped out of one reality in order to step fully into myself. Alone.

I live a different life now. Balanced. Fulfilled. In community. Steeped in nature. Creating, cooking, writing, documenting, music-making, traveling the world. All while pursuing my entrepreneurial ventures. I'm not a meditating monk, a solitary Sufi or a yammering yogi, but Spirit is everywhere.

I've lived the material that manifested into this treatise on transformation, or rather, the material lives *me*. I'm in a continual state of learning, growing, evolving, playing and gleaning lessons from an infinitely intelligent cosmos that co-creates its master plan for and with us as we navigate the vicissitudes of life.

I still face the consequences of my decision to depart the status quo. I experience setback and success, challenge and triumph, solitude and connection—the full spectrum of life's colors. I feel blessed and grateful for it all. "Things sometimes fall apart so they can fall together better."

This book is my offering. A giving-back for the plenitude with which I've been privileged. Life is a great unfolding adventure. Sharing insights garnered along the way is a form of honoring and celebrating the magnificent, magical, spontaneous universe from which it all arises.

HOW TO USE THIS BOOK

This book is a tool. An instrument. A vehicle for communicating a message of inspiration, unity and consciousness through vibrational symbols. The symbol of words.

While the messages in its pages, to paraphrase Kahlil Gibran, came *through* me, they are not *from* me. As the parents of children, progenitors of ideas, coordinators of movements, leaders of organizations, holders of space and intention we must, as stable bows, enable the living arrows launched through us to fly forth swiftly and far.

In other words, the efficacy of this material is dependent on you. Yes, *you*. Reading this right now. Because transmitting the teachings, wisdom and truth that resonates for you, uniquely for you, is imperative. To teach another is to really assimilate and synthesize the material for oneself.

You are an instrument of inspiration. Expressing your unique essence is the point of existence. The most powerful way to absorb anything is to express its resonance—in your terms—to someone else. To bring oxygen, nourishment, sustenance to another. That's how we become teachers.

Even though I wrote these pages, I can forget the lessons. Even though I know the truths, I can lose my way. I'm human. Just like you. Part of our humanity is having to learn and re-learn the lessons of our lives.

It is powerful and transformative to hear the principals return to me from another. I was in a state of disquiet when a reader reminded me of my center: *"Where are you hearted?"*

she asked. Hearing my words reflected back to me was a cogent prompt. Where *am* I hearted?

Since then, the concept has taken root. A daily calendar reminder alerts me to *heart* about—rather than *think* about—what I'm engaged with and where I'm directing my energy.

Like a potent trigger, sharing the lessons that stick can do as much for you as the person with whom you share them. Encouraging a confidante or friend, confederate or stranger is a way to inhabit the change you seek to make in your own life. Be the reminder. The tickler in the calendar. The font. The messenger. The muse. Because to inspire another is to inspire oneself.

This book is also a powerful divination tool. It responds to inquiry. Cradle it in your hands while contemplating a current challenge, choice or conflict. Ask for direction, confirmation or counsel. While holding this intention, flip to a page. Extraordinarily, wherever you land will present a relevant answer, a needed insight, a concise contemplation. Be it solution or reflection, encouragement or suggestion, the message leaping off the page will feel custom-tailored to your query. Perfect for you. Like magic.

When the principals shake things up or awaken something within you, go with it, capture your thoughts: write, journal, paint, create. Use the concepts, metaphors, phrases as leaping-off points. Let them trigger your imagination, stoke your spirit, light your fire to propel growth, transition, healing, evolution, revolution… in a word: *transformation*.

Become the instrument of your *own* success so that you can sound your horn or beat your drum or strum your strings or offer your voice to lend its essential note to the Universe, the one song (uni = one; verse = song) we all play together.

HOW TO SUCCEED ON PURPOSE

PURPOSE

Purpose is that which fills our cup while we fill the cup of another.

~ Truth

Purpose

A fundamental inner calling that
resonates as truth to our being.

The optimal use of our gifts, passionately performed.

When we're at our best,
while doing our best,
feeling our best while doing it.

That which in the doing is its own reward.

Acting in alignment with our truest selves.

Our life theme.

Our reason for choosing this human experience.

Accidentally... on Purpose

Life is an accident-free zone. The fact that you are holding this book in your hands and reading this sentence isn't by chance. If it happened by "accident" it is purposeful that you were directed to do so by divinely intelligent forces looking out for you.

In truth, the universe doesn't subscribe to accidents. There is meaning in everything. Even its accidents are on purpose. And that's what this book is about: *purpose*. Finding yours. And in so doing, finding success each and every day of your life.

You see, our purpose *is* purpose. Without purpose, life is meaningless. And without meaning, happiness becomes unattainable.

You're here for a reason. In fact, you *did* ask to be born. This book is about remembering why you chose to come into this life in this moment in time in this age of our evolution and in this body of yours, gifted with a set of wants and desires and the talent to fulfill them unique to you and you alone.

This book will help you to remember your purpose and to get back on the path you chose, you determined, you desired to explore when you arrived. You already know your purpose. Perhaps you forgot it or you forgot how to attune to it. Let's remember together...

Truth Serum:
Life is an accident-free zone.
Even its accidents are on purpose.

3

Being on Purpose

What does it mean to be *on* purpose? *Intentional.* And in alignment with one's highest aspirations for oneself and the Universe's highest aspiration for us. *Purposeful.* Purpose-full. Purpose-filled. Replete with purpose.

What holds us back from aligning with purpose? Myriad excuses: "It's the not the right time for this." "I can pursue my dream later." "I have too much going on right now." "What will my husband think, my partner think, my co-workers think, my children think, my community think?"

The answer to all those questions is "You're right." Whether you think you can or you can't, whether you have time for it or you don't, whether you're capable of it or you're not, you're right. More importantly, what holds us back from the imperative of purpose are the responsibilities and obligations we've placed upon ourselves, or rather, the contract we've accepted with society about what we "should" or "shouldn't" do. Rest assured, it's an agreement we can modify or discard whenever we want and we can redraft a new understanding with ourselves whenever we like.

A liberating truth to keep in mind when a dreaded "should" arises in your mind to keep you from your purpose: When you pursue your greatest desires and seek the highest, best fulfillment of who you are, what's best for you is actually what's best for everyone else around you.

It may not seem so at first. Your move to pursue your dream for yourself is bound to throw off the status quo. It might be inconvenient for others, but who said you were supposed to live life like a 7-11? You don't exist for the convenience of anyone else!

Choosing the path that serves your greatest purpose means you are being fulfilled by your work, sharing your greatest talents, role-modeling for others to pursue their highest calling, and in alignment with the cosmic forces that support you in all of your endeavors.

That it might upend the apple cart in the short-term is no reason not to do it. Breaking from patterns that don't serve you is a must in order to create new patterns that do.

Moving into intention from a place of unintentionality; moving into purpose from a morass of purposelssness; finding vision from a lack of clarity are imperatives of spirit and a precursor to joy, fulfillment, happiness, love, abundance, peace and ease.

In other words: Success!

Truth Serum:
When you are aligned with purpose, what's best
for you is what's best for everyone around you.

Purpose Narrows

My purpose is to light people up. To share my light with others so that they can themselves be illuminated from within. I'm not casting my light *on* them. I'm simply radiating my own incandescence and in so doing activating the incandescence of others.

In the Upanishads, a holy Hindu Vedic text, it is written: "No other knowledge is necessary in knowing one's self, for the Self is all knowledge; the lamp requires not the light of another lamp for its own illumination."

It's a clear mandate. In order to inspire others, to spark their fire, to inspire them to do, be, achieve their greatest selves, their highest aspirations, one must bring purpose to all of one's endeavors. No matter the form of transmission. Whether in word, speech, deed, interview, film, story, essay, poem, song... to reach people where they watch and read, live and breathe, listen and be.

"Shedding light" (on a subject, for instance) occurs when any of us acquires a plethora of insight, understanding, wisdom, experience, knowledge. When light is abundant, one can afford to shed the excess, project the plenitude, lavish the luminance. Hence, *shedding light* on the subject at hand.

For each of us, our journey of purpose is distinct. When we first align with purpose, it can feel like walking a tightrope. We must step carefully, consciously forward, keenly aware of our balance and our footing, keeping our eyes peeled on the step ahead.

As we begin to navigate our purpose with care and intention, the tightrope will widen to become, say, a narrow ledge or a balance beam. As we continue to honor the path, the initial narrows will broaden until, eventually, we are speeding down a ten-lane super-highway, taking in the view, scanning the road ahead, glancing in the rearview to have a gander at how far we've come, avoiding obstacles, road blocks and pot holes along the way — all while *on purpose.*

As for the Buddhas and Bodhisattvas among us, they are on purpose *all* the time. Their pathway is *all* of Creation and *all* things in Nature and *all* people and *every* interaction. Their very existence is purpose. Every breath, every movement, every action is intentional and aligned with their soul's mission such that it is all a meditation. Every thought, every word, every musing and contemplation, observation and insight, truth revealed and mystery uncovered or discovered. Which is why being on purpose feels so complete, whole, total. In its ultimate expression, purpose encompasses All of Life. And that's why it is expansive, not reductive. Inclusive, not alienating. Embracing, not repelling.

Even if we must initially reduce our purpose to a laser-focused beam of light and then walk that beam consciously and carefully, when we align with purpose, it expands to encompass all of our work, our play, our thoughts, our relationships, our conversations, our experiences — each and every moment of our lives.

If you live a life of meaning, then *everything* is meaningful. If you're life *isn't* a life of meaning, then you will attempt to create meaning out of the meaningless by projecting meaning onto objects, places, events and people.

When you are on purpose, nothing else really matters. Your happiness and fulfillment don't rely on anything external. If you are not on purpose, then the trappings of success are necessary to give you a sense of meaning. And those "trappings" keep us trapped.

The reason choosing purpose can feel narrow—even precarious—in the beginning is that if we've been off-purpose or if we've pursued that which is not aligned with our purpose, then those things, those foci, those people, that job, that community, those distractions… will fall away from us.

We will endure the crumbling of that which is known, that to which we have grown accustom. Creature comforts will fall like chaff and leave us seemingly with nothing — without our friends, our community, our work, our perks… our *stuff!*

Everything we thought mattered will drop away in order for us to concentrate on the things that truly do. And that's the incisive energy of purpose. Purpose is like a razor that cuts away that which does not serve us. It slices off that which does not foster the highest and best use of our gifts. Should we be cut or wounded with this razor, we must take it as part of our journey of illumination. Rumi observed that "the wound is the place where the light enters you."

Sometimes a shift to purpose results in us losing or discarding nearly all of our possessions. We may lose *everything* — whether by choice or force, disaster or divorce. We may find we need to start over with nothing but the breath in our lungs. But breath is life. And life allows for new beginnings.

Christ proclaimed that those to find The Way would "enter through the narrow gate." Maybe this is what he meant. Beginning again—with purpose—feels like stepping onto the narrows. We must take one small stride at a time on a slender path. A slender path with perhaps a narrow gate.

Even if we must edge slowly forward, sliding our feet and waving our arms to maintain our balance, our tip-toe efforts thicken, widen, bolster, and expand the narrows to become a vast field of possibility, experience, serendipity, synchronicity and, most of all, LOVE.

Love, love, everywhere you go, everywhere you look, gloriously omnipresent. And that's why aligning with purpose is so powerful, so fulfilling, so dynamic and enriching.

The *Law of the Parabola of Purpose* (expounded in a later volume) describes scientifically what happens when you are *on* purpose. It's how everything you perceive, all life events, every observation and exploit is directed back to your center, to the core of your being, where it is assimilated and integrated through the filter of purpose to be synthesized in the depths of your soul, at the nexus of your heart-mind.

In turn, everything that emanates *from* you is projected in a clear, bright, channeled beam of far-reaching collimated light. Like a parabolic beacon. A beacon of purpose.

It radiates from the absolute bullseye of your being. And you shine that majestic, infinite, loving, boundless, ever-reaching luminance wherever you aim your focus—to all corners of the Universe if it's your will to do so.

In this way, we can be light-shedding parabolas of illumination and magic. Unbounded fonts of energy, learning, and teaching — all directed, projected and amplified by purpose.

Purpose is your origin.

Purpose is your destination.

Purpose is your source.

Purpose is your birthright.

Purpose is your gift.

Purpose is your heart.

Purpose is your path.

Purpose is your light.

Purpose is your love

Purpose is your life.

Purpose is your destiny.

Purpose is as flexible a precept as they come. It is pliant, potent power. Purpose is limitless, expansive, inspiring, energizing, uplifting, progressive. It is myriad in its applications and as specific as it is universal.

Purpose dispels darkness.
Purpose sheds light on any subject at hand.
Purpose makes a great study partner.

Truth Serum:
The "trappings" of success keep us trapped.
Purpose sheds light on what truly matters.

Prioritizing Purpose

There are a million distractions. How can you tell when you're in the grips of one in a million? Ask yourself if what you're doing, what you're fixated on, what task you're enmeshed in, or those with whom you're entangled are furthering your purpose. If the answer is "no," then whatever has your attention is a distraction from what you SHOULD be doing, what you NEED to be doing, what you WANT to be doing, and what WANTS to be done by you.

We direct our creativity, command our powers of manifestation by what we pay attention to. We *are* paying for it. There's a cost to where we spend our time, where we focus our awareness. We are cashing in the powers of the Universe to manifest what we pay attention to.

Being *on* purpose is about putting our purpose at the center of our lives and clearing enough space around it to dedicate ourselves to that purpose. It means eliminating distraction. Neutralizing headwind. Allowing ourselves enough runway to get to takeoff speed; enough sky and fuel and thrust to achieve escape velocity.

When you do this, others might not understand. Count on them *not* understanding. You might be clearing your calendar, your agenda, your commitments, your friendships, your family. But it's all right. It's what you were meant for. It's what you *have* to do. If you want to Succeed on Purpose.

This isn't about shirking obligations, but about *shrinking* them. Realigning your life so that your priorities are in order. Ordered for a purpose. By purpose. *For* purpose.

It's making space to set up the target, fixing our aim at the bullseye and creating a launch corridor wide enough and long enough to build momentum, strength and focus to launch ourselves at it. Unwaveringly.

That is purpose-centered existence. And it's worth examining what we put at the center of our lives. What's off-target? What's on target? What life events or outcomes or results of our efforts hit the outer rings? Which actions strike the bull's-eye? Can you feel when things stray from the target? That feeling is what guides you. It's the biofeedback to readjust your aim.

The rub of archery is that when casting an arrow, if one's aim is off by just a few degrees upon release, the arrow will be off-target by even greater margin when the shot lands — or misses altogether. Therefore, we must calibrate our purpose by degrees. Gradually. Carefully. Paying attention to our aim; having clarity of focus; obviating distraction; absent obstacles; with a well-lit range of sight.

A comedian once joked about his humble upbringing, "We were so poor, we couldn't even *pay* attention." It's more true than we'd like to admit. We do pay for things with our attention. And it's either credited to our account, adds to our purpose and fulfillment, or it's a drain on our resources.

Our attention is our time, our focus, our life energy. And where attention goes, energy flows. So be sure that whatever you're paying for with your attention is worth it. That nagging suspicion that you're wasting your time, your energy, your precious resources, is telling you all you need to know.

When you have the feeling, "This is a waste of my time," it probably is.

Truth Serum:
Distraction costs us. That's why we must pay attention.
*   *   *
When we prioritize purpose we don't shirk
responsibilities, we shrink *them.*

I Can't... Yet

Whenever you say "I can't" you are asserting what is. Add a little "yet" and you open the door to what can be.

And yet... we rarely utilize "yet." It's a powerful way to allow what's possible. So often we feel trapped, hemmed in or forced into circumstances which arose from our own co-creation. There's the dreaded "I have to," the awful "I should," and the wearisome "I must."

"I can't" is the other end of the spectrum and equally limiting. When "I can't" do something it reinforces my current state of affairs. It asserts a limiting belief, though it may feel true at the moment. But as we know, everything is subject to change. To evolve. To transform. So "I can't *right now*" doesn't mean "I can't *tomorrow*" or "I can't *forever*."

Whatever limits us now, be it time, resources, acumen, skill, education, knowledge, assistance, inspiration... can and will be acquired if there is a desire to acquire it. So "I can't" is just a temporary expression of lack.

Dismiss the lack. Embrace abundance. The resources are there for "I can." The Universe has boundless creativity, infinite imagination and limitless energy. There are reserves enough for you. Even if you can't imagine how it's possible, the possible can and has imagined *you*.

"I can't... *yet*" swings the door of possibility open, allows in the radiant light of *I will* and ushers you into the field of pure potentiality that is *I am*.

Recant "I can't." Make it "I can't... *yet*."

I can transform "I can't." Why can't you?

Truth Serum:
Seem impossible? Say, I can't... <u>yet</u>.
The possible has already imagined you.

13

The Better Belly Button

"Know thyself" and "To thine own self be true."

These axioms have lasted the ages for good reason: they are wise, pithy and correct. One must know *oneself* before one can know another. One must recognize Truth in oneself before one can recognize Truth in another. To be *on* purpose, true *to* purpose is to be true to oneself. And when one is true to "thine own self," one is authentic.

We can recognize authenticity in another. When they speak from what they know. From their own life experience. From their inner wisdom. We see it. We know it. We feel it. Intuitively. Unconsciously. Accurately.

When someone is putting on airs, acting like they know what they're talking about or when playing at something they don't really have the experiential wisdom of knowing, then we can distinguish that. Our cues are nonverbal, vibrational, psychic. Their words and actions lack authenticity.

Inauthenticity is when you say "yes" when you mean "no." When you're feeling misalignment in your body, in the core of your being. And your being reflects that truth: you are being inauthentic despite your words or actions. The body and soul's natural state is authenticity. It's why children are so infectious: they are authentic. It's why we love pets: they are authentic in their affection, loyalty, playfulness and misbehavior. They don't know how to put on airs. They cannot be anything other than who or what they truly are. They aren't ironic. They aren't sarcastic. Purpose—like pets—can't lie.

Human beings are different. We start authentically enough, as babies and young children. And then we learn behaviors that lead us away from our Truth. We learn not to always speak from the heart. We're taught to say no when we want to say yes, or vice versa. We assimilate the lesson to hold back, to bite our tongue, to be reserved, to be well-mannered. Decorum notwithstanding, these societal practices—not all of them bad—teach us patterns of behavior that veer us away from a state of Truth. They move us out of touch with our veracity, our truest and most authentic selves.

So we have to learn to recognize when we are being inauthentic. When our thought-word-deed flow is incongruous. When there is dissonance between who we truly are and who we are pretending to be. When there is a degree of removal from what we are pretending to know or the part we are attempting to play.

Purpose is synonymous with authenticity. You can't be on purpose *and* inauthentic. Where authenticity is concerned—unlike with belly buttons—it's better to be an *outtie* than an *innie.* That is, in (authenticity) is out because you're on (purpose).

Truth Serum:
Where authenticity is concerned, in is out
because you're on (purpose).

| TIME |

The future is not the future when it comes.
When it comes it is the present.

~ Truth

The Time of Your Life

This is the time of your life. What time is it if it isn't?

There's no time like the present. There is—*literally*—no time but the present. What other time is there? As far as it concerns you and me and being alive, we have no choice, no alternative regarding time. It's a privilege, and perhaps our greatest challenge, to live the moments life offers to us as they come. To just live... present.

To live present as opposed to living *in* the present (day and age) is to be available for the here and now. In our bodies. In our awareness, observing. In a conscious state of mind.

This is the time of your life. There is no other time. Sure, there's the past, but that's a concept. And it's just past, you see? Past and gone. One second ago and a million years ago — same thing. You can't touch either or get the moment back.

Then there's the future, but that's slippery to grasp and impossible to know. We can project ourselves into the future in our mind's eye. But we're leaving the rest of us behind— our bodies, ourselves—and that's the best part: to really experience life, not just a projection of it, a memory of it, an idea, wish or hope for it. But actual, real, unfettered, off-the-hook, spontaneous life!

Ergo, this *is* the time of your life. There is no other time. Any other time of your life is just a concept. A wisp of perception. Time itself is simply a Divine construct to keep everything from happening at once.

And time is a conundrum. Even though it's a figment of our reality, which is to say a slice of the illusion, time has some hard and fast rules:

You can't save it.

You can't rewind it.

You can't slow it down.

You can't bank it.

You can't borrow it.

You can't loan it to someone else.

You can't bequeath it to your kids.

You can't save it up for a rainy day.

You can't get it back.

It marches ever onward. In one direction: Forward!

And it never retreats.

Sometimes time is a slog through molasses. Sometimes it moves at light speed. Sometimes it weighs so heavily on us that we feel it will drag us down an abyss where we'll perish. And sometimes it's light and airy like a Parisian croissant, effervescent as champagne or so buoyant and feathery that time even flies.

No matter what, time does what it does and we do what we do with the time available to us. So if you're thinking that some other time will be the time of your life, think again. *This* is the time of your life.

The camera is rolling. The director has already called "ACTION!" and this ain't a dress rehearsal.

The question is... are you ready for your close-up?

Truth Serum:
Right now is the best time
to have the time of your life.

Each & Every

Every day is a chance to start over. More than that, it's an imperative. We don't actually have a choice in the matter. We are starting from scratch each and every day. With everyone we meet, with everyone we thought we knew, with everything we think we know. Even with ourselves!

The sun rises. The day begins. The morning dew clings to blades of grass. The Earth starts afresh. Hope springs eternal.

The headway we thought we'd made is undone. The person we thought we knew is a different person than they were the day before. What was said or made or done, given or taken, achieved or accomplished in the past doesn't count—or perhaps counts *too* much—in the present. What's relevant… is that it's all *irrelevant*.

We thought we'd gotten somewhere. We thought we'd learned the lesson. We thought we'd earned a trust or gratitude, kindness or love, respect or adulation, hug or kiss or pat on the back. We deserve it, don't we? We worked for it. It was progress we could count on.

Well, we thought wrong. Because that was *yesterday*. What have you done for me *today*? What did you do to earn your place in the now?

Because even if we earned our stripes we still need stars to go with them. Even if we made the cut, we wake to face the next one. Each day a new slice. After a life of countless cuts, we move onto the next realm. Perhaps that's why it's "death by a thousand cuts." And no matter the deal we thought we'd cut, we don't have "final cut."

Welcome to square one. Each and every. Which is why all that matters, all that counts for anything is *right now*. And what we make of it. How we conduct ourselves. The attitude that motors our motion.

We can see this daily renewal both ways: as a chance to *get to* do things differently, to try again, to welcome a new beginning OR as a diurnal backpedal, a slide-back, a daily reboot where we *have to* start from scratch as if the slate were clean. Re-earning our place in the world. The respect we deserve. A seat at the table. The love of our lover. Over and over. Again and again.

Maybe we get credit for the thing we did before, for the trail we blazed or the accomplishments we assumed were inscribed on our "permanent record." Maybe there's some residual goodwill left in the cup. Or maybe it'll all count for nothing. No brownie points. No gold star. We have to earn it anew.

That's the itch of reality: scratching only delivers temporary relief. So start each day afresh. With the knowledge that yesterday might matter. Or it might not. Today is your chance to make the same mistakes or different ones. To dispense the same kindnesses or cruelties. To continue along the same path, to follow the same throughline or to make a change, try something else, choose an alternate route.

Today's a new day, a precious and delicate beginning. And even that's imprecise: it's a new *moment*. Moment to moment. Which is how so much can happen in a day — because twenty-four hours is a lot of moments stacked together. Our prerogative is to choose how we want to live each one whether we accept or deny each moment of every day is invented anew. Reborn. Remade. Begun afresh.

Now and always. Forever and ever. Again and again.

Each and every.

Whether we like it or not.

Truth Serum:
Each and every day—each and every moment—is a
chance to start over, afresh, anew.

Life Begins At...

Life begins at... 40. Or does it?

Is 40 the new 30? Does that make 50 the new 40? Or is it 60 that's the new 40? It's hard to tell. And harder to keep track. Seems we keep getting younger, in that whatever age we reach, we still feel ourselves, we still feel chipper and spry and like there's lots of living to do, lots of things to take care of, sights to see, places to go, people to meet, life to live.

Life actually seems to begin again and again each moment. As my father reminds me when we dialogue about future plans, goals, aspirations: "The present is your current starting point."

So life really begins... whenever we want it to.

We can tell ourselves that life begins when we have wisdom and experience and have learned enough from our mistakes not to make any mistakes going forward, but that's a lie. We will make mistakes. That's the way of life: trial and error. If you're not making errors, you're not trying hard enough because errors are made to learn from. And if we are learning, we are growing. And to grow is the ambition of living. We're either growing or receding; being born or dying; evolving or decaying.

You might be in your seventies with more than a few stories to tell the grandchildren in your lap as you retire into the lap of luxury. You're thinking "Now life begins."

Or perhaps you're in your mid-thirties with some not-so-gentle lessons under your belt thinking "life begins now."

Or you're about to have your first child and you're certain that parenthood is the point where "life (literally) begins now."

Or you're middle-aged and you've retired from one career, retired one marriage and you've decided to finally pursue that dream you've nurtured for decades now that you know who you really are: "Life begins now" you decide with certitude.

But what about that teenager about to get her driver's license? Or the one about to become a counselor at his summer camp? Or that senior who was just accepted early admissions to their first-choice college? Or the medical student about to complete her residency? For each of them, "Life begins *now*."

So when does life really begin?

Well, life begins when we think it does, when we believe it does, when we decide it's going to. Life begins as soon as we want it to or as late as we let it. Once we decide WHEN our life begins, THEN life begins.

So decide if life began the moment you arrived. Or as soon as you depart. For many that's precisely the life they're living for: the *afterlife*. But since you're alive right now, perhaps you'll choose to live the life you happen to be living at the moment. No matter *your* choice, life has already decided: It chose you the moment you arrived on its doorstep. Now *you* have the ability to choose. And, really, no matter what age you are, who you are, or when you are, you can always begin again.

Because all of our know-how and experience, our tools and problem-solving, our learning and savvy, our wonders and blunders, missteps and mistakes have prepared us for this very moment in the journey. They've primed us for this next phase of the adventure. For the next set of circumstances and challenges and opportunities. The next horizon to survey, the next mountain range to summit, the latest treasures to seek and fences to climb (and mend) on our way to the greener pastures we've pined for.

The decision of when is simple Zen: It's here and now. Each day we awaken can be the one when we decide: Today's the day! The first day of the rest of my life.

So life *does* begin at forty. Or fifty-six. At thirty-three. Or twenty-two. At ten. Or a hundred and one. The choice is yours. Only *you* determine when your own life begins. And if you decide that life begins right here, right now, *today*, then let me be the first to wish you... Happy Birthday!

Go get 'em, Tiger.

Truth Serum:
Life begins when we think it does, when we
believe it does, when we decide it's going to.

Momentary Houseguests

We're always on our way from this to that, from one spot to the next, in transit, en route. We don't think much of the time between here and there as we are just in-between locales. Running from one destination to another.

Yet the moments in-between are just as momentous as the moments that are not. Moments in-between are just as real. And as fleeting. Because the in-between isn't in-between anything. It's the whole enchilada. The moments in-between ARE our lives.

We're *always* in-between something: a rock and a hard place, the next big thing, our last success and the next one, a past failure and a future triumph. Each of the "big" moments are telling and impactful, but they are just moments. When we flit from here to there, from where we are to where we're going, from what *has* happened to what *will* happen, we miss out on what *is* happening. Now. Right now. Just NOW.

When we choose to live each and every moment as it comes, we're sure not to miss out on a thing. Because the big moments, the magic moments, the momentous moments are a product of all the moments that have led up to them and they inform every moment that follows.

The moments in-between are the very moments you've been waiting for. Don't leave any on your doorstep. Greet each one as it arrives, welcome it at the door, and usher it inside to revel in its company, however fleeting, because just as this moment takes its leave, there's another knocking, eager to be received, sure to never overstay its welcome.

Wouldn't it be nice if all houseguests were like moments?

Truth Serum:
<u>This</u> is the moment you've been waiting for.

Gift Receipt

Take your time. It's your time to take. No one can or should rush you. Your precious moments are no one else's to possess or to control, to cherish or to squander. Time is yours and yours alone. Who else does time belong to if not to you?

And as time is yours to make, take or break, to value, de-value, use or misuse, the question is... how are you *spending* your time? For time is currency. Far more precious than money, time is *the* treasure of human experience — of greater value than gold or gems, cash or coins. It is priceless beyond measure as it cannot be bought or banked, borrowed or loaned. We cannot move time from here to there. We cannot reserve time nor preserve time for more important affairs nor a rainy day.

Though wouldn't it be great to loan someone some time *sometime*? Or save time, earn interest on your time, put time away when you've got extra so that you can take time out (a time-out!) when you need it, when you've earned it?

And if you had some spare time, you could keep it in your pocket to whip out for a friend in need...

"Excuse me, do you have the time?"

"No. In fact, I need *more* time."

"Here, I've got *sometime* in my pocket. Why don't you have it?"

"Wow. Thanks for your time!"

"Any time."

Alas, time is priceless and fickle. It can't be saved, banked, loaned, stored, reclaimed, rewound, slowed or sped up. It tick-tocks inexorably, marking the milestones, an avalanche of annum, a multitude of milliseconds, a lifetime of coffee-spoons.

Whether quantified or glorified, meted out or measured, time marches on like the rhythmic thumping of soldiers' boots. *Boom-thump. Boom-thump.*

Though it sometimes whispers quiet musings like a gentle lover from a shared pillow. *Sweet nothings, sweet nothings.*

But time takes no prisoners, holds no quarter. It is exacting in its finitude: merciless, impartial and dispassionate.

So cash in on the rainy day, spend your precious minutes, gather ye rosebuds while ye may. Don't temper the gift by attempting to get it back in the box. Where time is concerned there are no give-backs, no returns.

Time is your present and yours alone to do with, to play with, to spend as you see fit. It's yours to squander, waste, toil or spoil. No one can bequeath you more and no one can steal it away unless you let them. We only have what's given to us. To make the most of it while we can. Time is a gift. Temporal and temporary.

Yours for the taking.

And there's no re-gifting.

It's all in the receipt.

Truth Serum:
Who does time belong to if not to you?

Divine Reflection

Being in the moment steadies the mirror in which all is reflected — the divine picture of our reality. If we're not in the moment, then we're holding up a jittery mirror that gives us a blurred sense of ourselves and a distorted image of life.

It can be a tremendous challenge to live in the moment, to live in the present when so much of our existence and what we think of as our inalienable selves is shaped and informed by the past. But the past is the past. We must let it go or we are watching yesterday's programs today and programming re-runs of the same for tomorrow.

Each moment is the accumulation of every moment that has led to this one. Being in the moment honors *all* the moments. We can't grasp one more than any other as each moment is fleeting, an evanescent flash in the fireworks of life.

Past, present and future are all contained in the moment. Which is why the present is your point of power. At the moment you are reading this sentence, everything in your past that has led up to now informs how you are thinking, feeling and responding to the idea of this sentence. How you decide to reject and discard, or assimilate and integrate, the idea expounded here into your future makes this present moment your latest beginning. As my dad, Sage, likes to say, "Now is your present starting point."

The fulcrum around which past, present and future revolve is now. *Right* now. *Just* now. And again... *now.*

If you get it, be present. Because we are all just wisps of consciousness having an ephemeral experience.

Truth Serum:
Being in the moment honors all
the moments that have led to this one.

All Time Awareness

Every creature on earth lives in rhythm to the moon, the stars, the planets, the sun and all other manner of celestial bodies that dictate and inform the seasons.

Even the Earth itself is in cadence with the patterns and revolutions of our solar system, our galaxy and the galaxies beyond. Everything alive is informed by a dance of the spheres. Humans alone are governed—via choice and collective agreement—by linear time.

By bringing our awareness to the moon in its arc overhead, the pattern of the stars as they swing across the night sky and the gentle evolution of the sun rising and setting, we can ground ourselves as creatures of the Earth and reaffirm our place in the Universe. As this immense dance of enormous bodies is choreographed by a Divine conductor, so, too, are the patterns and rhythms of our lives.

Burn the clock! Realign with celestial time. Become aware so that you aren't rushing around in a daze of temporal ignorance. Mankind only recently starting living by a different paradigm than the blade of grass, the tide, the migrating herd, the clutch of hens, the pod of dolphins, the kaleidoscope of butterflies, the loveliness of ladybugs. Despite our ignorance, we are still ruled by the same brand of time that governs everything else in the Universe.

The clock is ticking...

How are you going to spend your day?

Tick-tock. Tick-tock.

Truth Serum:
Human beings are bound and governed by celestial time — like everything else in the Universe.

| HEALING |

*Move from a state of despair
to a place of repair.*

~ Truth

Miraculous Function

How often do we thank our bodies for the miracle of their functionality? We appreciate our cars for their smooth operation and trouble-free performance, but how often do we thank our organs for doing their thing flawlessly and continuously on our behalf so we can continue to enjoy this human experience?

"Thank you, Heart," for beating without cessation.

"Thank you, Stomach," for doing all the hard work of breaking down my food as fuel.

"Thank you, Lips," for expressing what I have to say, for puckering appropriately when kissing, for sipping delicately, for slurping hot soup, for pursing when necessary and for not chapping inconveniently.

"Thank you, Lungs," for respirating despite my rare awareness of my breath, for automatically expanding during those times where I "forget to breathe," for infusing my cells with the oxygen of life and exhaling the CO_2 that my system no longer needs, for connecting me with my own spirit through inspiration.

"Thank you, Eyes," for clear seeing and for being the portal to my soul so others may see the light within me.

"Thank you, Brain," for working tirelessly to manufacture thoughts that might be of use, for tapping me into memory and creativity and speech and expression and enabling balance and movement and managing metabolic function and for bringing intelligence to problem-solving and creative thinking and for awareness of the universe and making sense of my place in it.

"Thank you, Feet," for carrying me where I need to go, for blazing trails where others fear to tread, for carrying my weight, for catching me as I fall forward from step to step, for transporting me in times of fright at breakneck speeds for kicking and jumping and hopping and skipping and climbing stairs and mountains and monumental distances that all start with a single step.

"Thank you, Bones," for protecting me, giving me support in all things and all ways, for the fortitude to carry the mass of all other viscera, for giving me form and function, prominent cheeks and elbows and tarsals, metatarsals and phalanges, and for encasing my marrow in the deepest and most protected part of your inner vessel.

This body that is a vehicle for spirit is more miraculous in its function than anything that we could ever invent. It's self-regulating, self-healing and autonomously operating.

Whether evolved, architected or divinely designed, it is miraculous and perfect and as profound in its complexity and uniqueness as the cosmos, as the living and breathing Earth, and any complex organism from the mighty redwood tree to the delicate hummingbird to the grandiose elephant to the humble bumble bee to the elegant dolphin.

We contain worlds within us as spectacular and awe-inspiring as the worlds outside of us. We are literally made of stardust. Give thanks to the stars from which we arose and to the cosmos to which we return when our time in these spirit-bodies comes to an end.

Even when our bodies cease to be, we don't. When our bodies expire, our spirit doesn't. And so we're living within a temple of flesh and blood and bone. And that temple is holier than any other wrought by Humankind. It is a temple of spirit, a temple of Purpose, a temple of the Divine. If this temple isn't deserving of our gratitude, then what is?

The only time we really turn our attention to our bodies or to its individual parts is when something's "wrong" with them. And, really, that's the body part's call for our attention, for some acknowledgement of it operating nominally without any praise or attention... ever.

Our parts are just like us: essentially happy to play their role, to do their bit, but when they (like we) get overworked, ignored or out of tune, poisoned by a toxic environment or viral interlopers, they break down, rebel, cease to operate at their optimum.

Functionality goes sideways so that they (like we) get the attention they deserve because each part serves an essential function. The whole system can't operate optimally unless each component does. Like us, our parts and pieces require recognition and praise to get back up to speed. Or the whole system slows down. Or breaks down.

So be thankful for this flesh suit while you have it. It's more refined, infinitely more robust and better sewn than any couture attire designed by Armani, Dolce & Gabbana, Gucci or Versace. It's bespoke—custom-made, one-of-a-kind—just for you. Divinely-tailored from the quantum fabric of creation by the Universe itself.

When God poured you, he broke the mold. So love your body while you have it. Revel in your unique temple. Give thanks every now and then to each of its parts and pieces.

Praise its totality, the wholeness of being that *is* you. For your body carries precious cargo on board: your spirit. Revere it to connect with your own Divine nature. We transport *ourselves* when we honor that which transports *us*.

Truth Serum:
Give thanks for your body, divinely-tailored from the
quantum fabric of creation by the Universe itself.

Be a Healer

When we work on purpose—or play on purpose, for that matter—we become healers for others. Like playing the right note on a finely-tuned instrument.

For what is healing? Healing is removing impediments, revealing truths, piercing the veil, providing insight, allowing awareness, making permission possible so that others can *heal themselves.*

Healers don't heal anyone, per se. "Healers" remove blockages in understanding or awareness whether physical, emotional, intellectual, energetic or spiritual. Once those blocks are removed and the pathways opened, it enables one's own healing energies to flow.

Doing our life's work — living our theme, leaving our spiritual legacy, playing on purpose — makes us healers in our own right because we are clearing the way for those touched by us, by our message, influence or energy to heal.

As each of us steps into our gifts, sharing them with others, thus the world shall be healed.

Truth Serum:
When we remove understanding's impediments and
clarity's sediments, we allow others to heal themselves.

The Purpose of Suffering

Suffering's purpose is its cessation. Plain and simple. Why do bad things happen? Why is there suffering in the world? So it can end. Suffering is a sacrificial lamb, giving itself up to the cause of its own demise. Suffering's sole reason for being is so we can determine how to end it.

Suffering has purpose. Just like you. It's single-minded mission is to flag what needs attention, what needs to change, what needs to be ameliorated, what needs to be cured, helped, assisted, rescued, solved. All of the causes of suffering are problems, issues, conditions crying out to be addressed. Suffering is a flame that *wants* to be extinguished. A weed that *wants* to be pulled at the root. A case that *wants* to be closed. Suffering desires to meet its end.

Suffering is *insufferable*. When we are suffering we hope, wish and pray for our misery to cease. No one wants to endure it nor do they want it to endure. Therefore we move in the direction of positive change and problem solving. Suffering is a pre-condition for something better.

How do we alleviate our suffering? If it's pain in our bodies, we seek medical attention. If it's pain in our hearts, we seek the comfort of family, friends, loved ones, a new companion. If it's life circumstances, living conditions, famine, oppression, persecution, profound dissatisfaction... we are moved to find solutions. As quickly as we are able.

Suffering is extreme. It's more than malaise or discomfort, more than sadness or loneliness. Suffering is an exacerbated state of mind, body and circumstance that makes suffering's *cause* a priority to deal with. Resolution is mandatory. Urgent. When we see suffering or feel suffering ourselves we want it to end. When we see others suffering we desire to help them end it. That instinct is our humanity. Our empathy. Our active listening at work.

Our desire to alleviate the negative forces in our purview is the striving of collective consciousness. The spirit of Humankind is an instinct to aid each other because of our innate and intuitive awareness that we All are One. Helping one of us is helping all of us. For suffering to persist, all we have to do is ignore our inherent will to do something about it.

When we've reached a state of suffering ourselves, we're all-in on the downside. Things might go from bad to worse, to greater *degrees* of suffering, but suffering is the klaxon sounding, the fire alarm ringing. Our red alert. We need to do something about it and fast. Put our heads together and figure out a way. Get some help.

Suffering is the Universe's way to focus our energy on a problem that needs our personal or collective attention. The causes that give rise to it must be investigated, understood and dealt with in order to stop the corollary of suffering.

The sole purpose of suffering *isn't* to make us stronger. It's purpose is to find the cure, the salve, the balm, the healing combination for you or another's struggle and put an end to it. *Suffering's purpose is its cessation.*

When bad things happen and inflict wounds that cause suffering—Why? Why me?!—remind yourself that the primary reason for your suffering is so that you can learn how to end it. Once you do, not only will you be healed, but you will be empowered by your ability to do so and emboldened to face the greatest of challenges in your life.

God doesn't throw anything at you that you don't have the power to handle, the power to surmount, the power to heal. Once you've proven to yourself that you can do it, you are empowered to help others. And to inspire them.

In this way, suffering has purpose. Suffering fosters healing. Suffering commands attention. It narrows focus. It heralds change. It presages solution, relief and joy.

Even suffering needs its champions.

Truth Serum:
Suffering's purpose is its cessation.

Healer, Heal Thyself

When we are in tune with our Inner Voice, aligned with our purpose, on our PLR ("Path of Least Resistance," as my dad would say), then we are doing healing work. What sharpens our tools, our instinct for what we do, our narrative of trust and authority, is a sense of "knowing."

And what is knowing? An intuition of truly, deeply understanding another's suffering, empathizing with another's experience and being able to advise, guide and help them heal because we, ourselves, have been where they've been, walked where they have walked, and emerged from the fire. We can be guides because we have been there ourselves. It is this conviction that is construed as *wisdom* by others. It can be sensed. Beyond intelligence, beyond intuition, wisdom is a tacit recognition in another of true knowing.

When we recognize someone as an "old soul," we sense their innate wisdom; a profound understanding that can only be borne from experience. When we are in the presence of an old soul, we know it. They harbor something deep within them. Even if it's a child—an infant—we can recognize it. Something tells us this being has *lived*. That he or she has a sense of knowing drawn from life itself — whether this life or previous ones.

How is that wisdom garnered? Through awareness — of life's experience, its vicissitudes of joys and sadnesses, celebrations and mournings, triumphs and defeats, health and sicknesses, lives and deaths.

When we question *why* we have to endure different challenges, *why* we have to solve problems, overcome heartbreak, heal ourselves of ailments... we're questioning the purpose of the life experiences from which we draw our knowledge. The very material that fuels our soul growth.

Wisdom garnered from living can be likened to skydiving or to having children: For those who've done it, no explanation is necessary; for those who haven't, none will suffice. We lived it. We learned it. We're wiser for it.

To know "it" is to have experienced "it." And that makes us all better healers. That's when we can truly connect with others on their own parallel journeys. We can reassure, guide, and ultimately help them to heal *themselves* because we have ourselves been healed.

This is how our individual lives connect us with everyone else's singular being. And why we need to embrace the uniqueness of our own experience. Because even though we are one-of-a-kind, wisdom is what unites us. Wisdom is what expands the universal well of consciousness.

We add our gathered knowledge, like precious droplets, to the infinite spring from which we all drink. A well that feeds and hydrates and slakes our thirst. As the magnitude of our inquiry grows, so does the wisdom well's capacity to nourish us, to heal us, and thus to heal the world.

Truth Serum:
Wisdom garnered on our healing path inspires
others to cultivate their own healing wisdom.

Hurting & Healing

It's a cycle. Never ending. We are in a constant state of wounding ourselves—emotionally, physically, spiritually—from one source or another and then healing ourselves. Again and again.

Hurting and healing. We are in a perpetual state of repair, of maintenance, of growth and recovery — that's our cycle of life. From neglect to nurture. From unloved to love. From absent-minded to whole-hearted.

We are continually refreshing that which spoils. Replenishing the shelves. Extending our virtual shelf life. And so it goes until we expire. We are never done. It's never over. Until *we* are.

Till then we're in a constant state of being born or dying. Of hurting and healing. Of ascension and decadence. Of creation and destruction. And so it is with the Universe.

Welcome. Jump on in. The bathwater's luke. Soon to run cold. But it can—and will—be heating up again. Once we add some flames to the fire. Some coals to the blaze. Stoke the ashes from which the Phoenix has just arisen.

Be patient with these magical creatures—with you, with me, the Phoenix. Give 'em just a sec. They were ashes only moments ago. They're just getting warmed up.

Truth Serum:
Our cycle of life is one of perpetual repair and
maintenance, growth and recovery, death and rebirth.

Add Repair to Your Repertoire

When you repair something — a situation, a thing, a person, a state of being — you are pairing it with something *again*. To *repair* is to pair anew.

But with what is the broken element being paired? When it's a relationship, for example, or a bodily organ? Does it reconnect to itself like a fractured bone? What about a busted transmission? Or a shredded document? A broken family? A cleft heart? A severed limb? A punctured tire? A shattered dream? A fence in need of mending?

When we *repair* anything, it is with the Divine. We are reconnecting, reacquainting, renewing its association with a Divine state of being.

The ground state of the Divine is perfect, whole, healthy, light, free, bountiful, limitless, omnipresent and perfect. When something is broken, severed, damaged, diseased or in need of repair, it requires realignment with the state of energetic ubiquity that is Divine Source energy. It requires attunement with Loving Consciousness, which can mend, heal, fix, solve, ameliorate, alleviate, restore, remake, repair... *anything*.

By holding the intent to reacquaint something with the Divine, you won't be in despair, but a state of repair. You'll have added "repair" to your repertoire.

Truth Serum:
To repair something is to reconnect it
with its Divine state of being.

Faith Healing

It's all about Faith. Even for the faithless.

Those without faith don't realize it, but their choice *not* to have faith or to reject faith is a function *of* Faith. We can't get away from Faith. To be faithless is a choice that demonstrates the courage of one's own convictions and therefore an act of faith *in ourselves*. Which is what Faith is really about.

Faith in *oneself* translates into faith in the Universe, in the Creator, because we, by definition, by design, by the very notion of our presence in Creation, are a product of Divine energy, expression and love. One's belief in oneself is a confirmation of one's connection to All That Is, to the Divine, to the inexpressible, the ineffable, the Supreme Ultimate. Faith in oneself is *an act of faith in the Universe*. A receipt of trust. Listening to our Inner Voice, our All-Knowing, All-Guiding, All-Purpose Inner Voice.

Try to reject Faith and it creeps up on us. Life throws us lessons over and over again until we learn to trust ourselves. Who else to trust if not oneself? And in trusting oneself, in having faith in oneself, we cast a vote for faith in the Divine.

When people say they have "faith" or that their "faith is strong" we might interpret that as religious fervor or spiritual belief. Yes, and… faith is much more than that. It imbues everything. It's everywhere. Infused into everyone.

Faith has many permutations, takes myriad forms and has gradations of all sorts and colors. In the end (as in the beginning), faith is our e-ticket for the roller coaster ride that is the human experience. Wherever we initially bought our fare, we had faith we were in for the ride of a lifetime.

Being born into this world, onto this plane of existence, was a huge leap of faith. The very act of birth is a miraculous expression *of* faith. A belief that somehow lovemaking and the conjoining of a seed of life from each parent multiplies into the incredible form of a human being within the womb of its mother.

We are birthed naturally into the world with fingers and toes in the right places; brain, heart and lungs developed and working as they should; with an infinite, impregnable, indescribable soul on board. Birth is the most tremendous act of faith there is. Acting with confidence that this process will somehow take hold and result from the intention to have a child is the greatest act of faith in our lives.

And that's where it begins. Where WE begin. Where it ALL begins: with miraculous conception! A luminous event spawning trillions of mitotic cell divisions to result—voilà!—in an extraordinary, magical human baby birthed into the world. And that's our *starting point*.

So if the act of giving *birth to life* is about faith, then how can *life itself* be about anything other than Faith? What else could it be about, pray tell?

I'm sure you can come up with something.

I've got faith in you.

Truth Serum:
In the end, as in the beginning, it's all about Faith.

| HUMANITY |

It's Humankind not Humancruel.
Embrace the former, eschew the latter.

~ Truth

The Human Condition?

What exactly is the human condition? Being human isn't a condition that can be ameliorated with a salve. It's not a temporary state of being (while on Earth). And being human *isn't* conditional. It's not predicated on anything. You don't need to qualify. There's no credit check. No application process. If you're reading this, you *are* human. Conditions have been satisfied. You're pre-approved.

Being human is a state of being. You came into this time and place for a reason knowing full well what you were getting yourself into. You *did* ask to be here. Your soul knows why, and it knows what you are here to accomplish. And the way to accomplish anything and everything is through love. So radiate love, be love, be *in* love. That's human truth. Love reaffirms our humanity. Unconditionally.

Being human is not a condition that requires a cure. Best not to think of it as a "condition" in the first place. Like it's something we were diagnosed with and wonder how we contracted it and how we might cure it. It's our regard for it, our perspective on it, that demands a new prescription.

Being human isn't something with which to come to terms, but something to embrace, to celebrate! It's who we are. What we are. How we are. No elixir will remedy it. No balm will heal it, nor make it disappear, nor fade away, nor reverse its effects. Nor should we want it to.

Solve your perspective, don't salve your condition. You're human. Welcome to the club. Membership has its privileges.

Truth Serum:
Being human isn't "conditional." Don't salve
your condition. Solve your perspective.

Your "U" You

When you ask the question "Who am I?" who is the you whom you ask?

You might ask out loud. You might urgently inquire. You might just be curious. Perhaps you're at a crossroads. Perhaps you're at the end of the road. But who are you asking? You're not asking "out there." You're not expecting a reply from outside of yourself. You're asking within. But not your surface self, your skin-deep self. You're asking a profound part of you. A hidden you. A soulful you. The ineffable, untouchable, inexplicable you.

And when the you that is the *Ultimate You* speaks, it does so with a silent shout. More quietly than a pin-drop, but in a booming whisper so that, miraculously, you can hear it. And only you. Because it's *your* Inner Voice. Your inner cognition that resides at the center of your being. In your Heart-Mind. It responds to your question. It tells you who you are. Without hesitation, reluctance, or prevarication.

Because your Inner Voice knows the boldest, broadest, most complete and idealized version of you. Your Ultimate You. Yes, your "U" You. From its lofty, ideal state of infinite knowing and familiarity with the absolutely best version of you, your U You will tell you who you are. In terms comprehensive and comprehensible.

Your U You offers the words, the wisdom, the guidance to keep you on track so that you can direct your consciousness toward the macro, the Big Picture: the largest frame of who you are without getting lost in all the nagging details. It's who we see when we pull away from all the mundanities of life, all the tasks, all the dramas, the ups and downs, the sicknesses and recoveries, the news, war, famine, the sticker price before rebates, our credit rating, our retirement savings, our mortgage application, our title at work, our age, shoe size, IQ, our permanent record... Anything that evaluates and quantifies and measures us. It's all done away with and discounted when your Inner Voice speaks. Because the Ultimate You gives you the bottom dollar. The baseline. The foundation. The skinny. The 4-1-1. Unadulterated. Without editorializing the content. It's the most encapsulated, crystallized and concentrated version of who you are, who you can be, who you were meant to be. And it knows your greatest hits before you've even written them!

It's you the way the world *wants* to see you, but may not know it yet. The way the Universe sees you, as if with X-ray vision. The way the Creator sees you, in perfect 20/20. With the greatest intentions for you in hand... so listen up!

How does your Inner Voice respond when you pose the question, "Who am I?"

Well, your Inner Voice doesn't speak in the Second Person. It doesn't say, "You are..." It responds in the "I am..." Your Inner Voice already knows to whom it speaks. And because it speaks about oneself, it doesn't bother with sentences. It's as pithy and punchy as can be. It will respond with as few words as possible to convey its message with crystal clarity. Perhaps with a single perfectly-chosen word. Because it wants you to get it. Get it?

We consider our bodies to be *us*, but our bodies are *not* us. The body we associate with so strongly is just a framework, a temple for us to play in. Your Inner Voice is the you whom you ask when you ask who you are. It speaks from holistic totality. It is the *real* you — untouchable, unknowable, immutable, impenetrable, ever-evolving, ever-conscious, eternal.

It's all right to converse with your Inner Voice, to have a dialogue about who you are and who you feel you are. If you are quiet enough and attentive enough, you will receive all the answers—to any question—because your Inner Voice knows. It knows you. Because it IS you.

By asking and receiving an answer, it can inspire you to direct your consciousness, your thought patterns, toward fulfilling the promise and potential of the Ultimate You rather than being occupied with extraneous details.

As a matter of practice, ask yourself, "Who am I?" And listen quietly for the response that comes. When your Inner Voice responds don't judge it, label it, or think about it. Just receive the answer. Ask again if you like. And again. And again. The answer will keep coming. It may change over time as you age, evolve and refine your purpose, but in this moment it will be consistent and insistent.

Ask later in the day and the same answer will arise because our Inner Voice is steady and steadfast, reliable and resolute, tenacious and truthful. And it's right. That's right. It *is* right. It is always, always, always and forever on the mark.

According to the yogis and the gurus and the Bodhisattvas (enlightened beings), your U You is like the movie screen upon which the film of your life is projected. Drama doesn't affect the screen, explosions don't burn it, currents don't soak it, blood doesn't stain it. When the show's over and the lights come up, the screen remains, blank and unperturbed, ready for the next tale, for the next set of players.

The same is true for your Ultimate You. The comedy, the drama, the horror, the victories, the highs and lows, the journey to the innermost cave, all of it is a fleeting dance of light and sound, a convincing illusion that engages us and thrills us and breaks us down and dejects us and tears us apart and puts us back together again and lifts us up and fires our imagination and creativity and wonderment. And for all the highs and lows, we wouldn't trade them for the world.

Life's great drama and unexpected plot twists keep us so riveted, so engaged, that we forget the screen, forget the theater and lose ourselves in the created reality that isn't at all real, that exists for entertainment purposes only, for the benefit of learning and growth and remembering the true nature of things. The nature of our own Nature: that we are infinite, Divine and—just for a moment—human.

And then the story ends. And we leave the theater unharmed, whole and full with the benefit of the experience and the memory of the moments we'll carry with us—forward, onward, into the next adventure.

Just don't forget the popcorn!

Truth Serum:
Your Inner Voice knows. It knows you. Because it is you.

Don't Pooh-Pooh Your Gift

We can all be a bit modest about facing and embracing our "gifts." Well, maybe *most* of us are modest.

"You're gifted," you might have said to another.

"You have a gift," another might have said to you.

And what's your response? Do you diminish the compliment? Pooh-pooh the acknowledgment? Shrink back or retreat from your own natural talent?

Here's the rub: your gift is not for you. It's actually God's gift to the world. It's the Universe's gift to itself. You're simply the messenger, the vehicle, the instrument for its delivery. Your gift is meant to be shared!

When you're "gifted" you've been blessed. And blessings are endowments multiplied when spread freely, generously and profusely. Talents are meant to be expressed, performed, implemented, promulgated and enjoyed—in joy—by others. Your gift is actually everyone else's gift. Not your own.

To deny your own gift—be it peace, ease, grace, voice, dancing, driving, flying, philosophizing, investigating, relating, painting, sculpting, broadcasting, building, networking, experimenting, connecting or expressing—is to deny others a gift *they* deserve from which *they* would derive great benefit. And who wants to take someone else's present from under the tree?

Recognize your gift as a gift for the world, not an indulgence to reject, nor a talent to pooh-pooh, nor a propensity from which to withdraw. Your unique, innate, genuine genius belongs to everyone. In its giving, you are the biggest beneficiary. For as satisfying as it is to receive, it's an even greater pleasure to bestow a present upon another. So give your gift to the world. Don't be shy. It's the greatest gratuity you can give yourself.

And if you think you are God's gift… you're right! Your life *is* a gift. And your talent lies at the center of it. Don't be afraid to tear into the wrapping paper to get to it.

We all deserve your present even if you feel you don't.

Truth Serum:
Your gifts are not your own, they are gifts
intended to be shared with the world.

Everything a Guru

Everything and everyone is our teacher, hence, our guru. ("Guru" translates from Hindi as "teacher.") If we shift our view from seeing obstacles as barriers to our success and instead view them as opportunities to grow then we realize a huge and essential portion of our education is *free!*

Most of us see difficult people, challenging circumstances and unfavorable conditions as roadblocks to our success or joy but when we shift our perspective to see the impasse as the *teacher*, it transforms thoughts of sabotage into gratitude and opening. We train ourselves to see the gift in the "grift."

Obstacles give freely of themselves. When we bump up against one and offer thanks instead of aggravation, it can transform the roadblock into a block party. That barrier might have saved you from a *worse* fate. It might teach you how to avoid obstructions like it in the future. It might impart a necessary dose of patience. It might instruct you how to go with the flow.

We all experience challenges. Those challenges invariably become the vehicle for our maturation and growth. When we are confronted by an impasse, we don't like it, but it forces us to find a solution. A way around, over or through. Another way of doing something that empowers us to better confront similar types of challenges down the road. Through tests, we grow. And build confidence in our ability to handle challenge, confrontation and stress with aplomb.

Like a sensei who strikes his student with a bamboo pole to teach him to sit still while in meditation. Or who commands an apprentice to attempt an impossible feat to prove she can do it. Our teachers help free our minds of limitation so that we grow to recognize our own power.

Are you currently facing a difficult personality type that seems hell bent on denying your every request? Resisting your rise? Curtailing your charge ahead?

Haven't you been there, done that? If you've seen it before, you'll see it again, but you can and should be armed with experiential tools to get the best result despite them.

The stick-in-the-mud administrator? We've seen her before. And we know how to handle her. Better yet, how to handle our reaction to her. We don't let her get the best of us. We don't cave in to the curmudgeon.

She doesn't know that she's your guru, but *you* know it. Just because someone doesn't *know* they are your teacher doesn't mean you should deny yourself the lesson they have to offer. And it also doesn't mean you have to live *with* them. *"Leave the teacher, take the lesson."*

We've all had that first grade teacher who tore the erasers off the end our pencil with her sharp, painted nails so we couldn't erase our mistakes, but instead had to circle them and write them over.

We've all had the fourth grade teacher who would assign us in-class reading and then pick her nose and eat it while she read the newspaper.

We've all had the high school English teacher who had it out for us where nothing we wrote would satisfy, not even our treatise on the impenetrable *Beowulf*.

We've ALL had educators like this. Right?

These were our *official* teachers. And we either grew or shrank from the experience. We rose to meet their challenge or we lived with resentment. They taught us something about life, about handling and confronting difficulty and about ourselves.

But we're not in second grade nor high school anymore. Perhaps our teachers are still there, imparting their lessons to a new crop of students. But we've moved on. We've left those instructors behind. We transcended that experience even though at the time it dominated our world and went on forever. But it was fleeting. Ephemeral. Like all things in life.

But the memory isn't. And whatever lesson we took from the experience has shaped the rest of our lives in some way, large or small. If we learned well, we left the teacher, but took the lesson. The teacher is gone, the teaching remains. This adjustment in our attitude toward daily challenges can help to infuse us with a pacifying wisdom about the nature of things.

Leave the teacher. Don't let them dominate our reality. Don't react to their methods. Don't let their attitudes pollute our biosphere. *Take the teaching.* Don't deny ourselves the lesson by discarding both the teacher *and* the wisdom.

Often our greatest teachers—those from whom we learn what we *don't* want and who we *don't* want to be—are unaware of their impactful role. What a loss, really, that the most efficacious gurus are oblivious to their own import. Such is the irony of the universe and a "people paradox," that the most unpleasant of us miss out on the satisfying pleasure of their own heuristic gift bestowed upon another.

To see our opponents as sages and our obstacles as opportunities ameliorates adversity. It defuses heated situations and transforms each hurdle and hardship, threat and fret, every roadblock and crackpot, into our teacher.

Everyone and everything a guru.

Truth Serum:
When we make obstacles our teachers—greeting gurus with gratitude—we transform roadblocks into block parties.

The Same Boat

It's a human imperative to know that we are not solo sailors, that we're not crewing the craft alone, that we're not solitary passengers. It's comforting, reassuring and life-affirming to know that there are others with us in the same boat.

Especially in times of difficulty. When the going gets tough. When we deal with the infinite tests that mark our existence as human beings, as when we step to challenge, face crises, confront our fears, lick our wounds, mourn, fall back, retreat, or evacuate.

The same boat is how we rally support to charge ahead. Connecting with others who feel the same way at the same time, who experience our same pain, heartbreak, fear, or uncertainty, makes all the difference. Whether fire, famine or flood; volcano, earthquake or hurricane; act of terror, act of war, or act of God; whether awash in tides of sorrow, or drowning in tsunami tides; while facing the shock of tragedy, collective sorrow, guilt, remorse, or shame.

We must know that we are not alone. Not bereft of companionship and community. We need compatriots who endure the same hardships, tackle the same challenges, handle the same disappointments, confusion, indecision, cope with the same grief, loss, or uncertainty.

No one wants to be the "man overboard." When we see someone tossed into the drink, we throw 'em a life-preserver. We reel that castaway in. Call it support, call it community, call it solidarity, but a flailing swimmer needs a rescue vessel. Especially when facing the unknown.

Finding ourselves in the same boat galvanizes us, lifts us up, makes us feel better about what we're feeling. Especially when we don't know what to do, how to plot our next move, how to prepare ourselves, brace ourselves, embolden ourselves.

We muster mettle through mutuality. We coalesce confidence through camaraderie. We chart a course, we trim the sheets, we catch a wind that fills our sails, when we realize we are not alone. That we're paddling, sailing, gliding, rowing, puttering, crewing, helming... similar ships, common crafts, identical vessels. In other words, the same boat.

Shipmates bolster courage. Courage begets hope. Hope is buoyant. It helps us rise. And that's why hope can float the boat.

Truth Serum:
When we find others in the same boat it lifts spirits, fills sails and raises hopes, which keeps the boat afloat.

| SUCCESS |

Succeed by being successful.

~ Truth

Success

The synchronistic, effortless and ample replenishment of
resources—spiritual, material, energetic—that
support the fulfillment of our purpose.

Our most enhanced version of life and well-being
coupled with our maximum contribution to the world.

Giving, contributing, adding *more* to Creation
than one takes from the contributions,
additions and gifts of others.

Success Isn't Google Mappable

What we're brought up to believe is that success is a point on the map and that there is a clear and direct route to reach it.

Why be Lewis and Clark and blaze new trails to get where we're going when others have already navigated the terrain? We're told that success can be ours if we just follow these step-by-step, turn-by-turn directions. We're sure to arrive at our destination. Google's mapped it. Google knows better than we do. Google knows everything!

And then reality hits: traffic snarls, construction delays, street cleaning, accidents, rubber-necking, cul-de-sacs, dead-ends, wrong turns, detours. Wait a minute... Google said *this* way was the *right* way. But I haven't arrived. This isn't success. I'm not rich! I'm not happy! What gives, Google? I want my money back (even though the app is free)!

As we are destined to discover, success is *not* a point on a map. There's no single way to arrive there. Success isn't even the same—nor synonymous—for everyone. Therefore it's always a unique locale. *Success is when we feel rewarded by a system, community, or environment that acknowledges and validates the talents and contributions we uniquely offer in service to others and the world.*

We're in a place in global society where success has become synonymous with financial abundance. Something is successful as long as it makes money. Even if the quality is poor. Or the product failed. Or someone lied to get it. Or cut corners in the process. Or destroyed people's lives, people's jobs, people's health. Or inherited the money. Absconded with the money. Or even if the money is funny.

But is that *your* criterion? Is that how you gauge success? What if you became an internet millionaire—or billionaire, for that matter—in your 20's or 30's? Is your ambition to just make *more* — for another 50, 60, 70 years? Or will other measures of achievement evolve?

Will your success be about elevating consciousness? Getting elected? Shifting the culture? Creating thought leadership? Enhancing academia, public health or housing? Being of service? Making an impact? Thriving off the grid? Aggregating a following? Saving lives? Preserving the environment? Having fun? Raising a family? Going to space? Traveling the world? Cultivating optimal health? Feeling fulfilled every day?

Success might be *externally* defined, but it's an *internal* triumph. We often take our measure of success against the yardstick of another's achievements even though their success cannot inhibit, take away from, nor compare to our own.

By *outside* measure, someone might perceive you to be successful, but that feeling of accomplishment, of a job well done is known unto you and you alone. You know when you feel it because it fills you up, energizes you, puts you in the universal flow of resources, taps an infinite wellspring of creativity, ideas, inspiration and energy. Quite simply, it makes you happy. It imbues you with joy. And delivers a sense of fulfillment of your purpose.

Contrast this to feeling the *absence* of success. Not failure, per se, but success's *lack*. It is empty, enervating, draining. It delivers doldrums, imbues one with lethargy and disappointment. It's a feeling that we can do better, that we deserve better; that we should earn more, be more.

By any measure, our feeling of success emanates from *within*. It's why successful people project success: their inner glow radiates outward to their environment affects others in their radius. They feel rewarded by life and, in turn, reap life's rewards.

Success is an inside job, so the quest, fundamentally, is about seeking for oneself. We must hunt *outwardly* to fulfill our potential while pursuing our greatest joy *within*. When we define success honestly for ourselves and align with a reward system that values *our* values then success gleams from the inside.

If we are misaligned with a reward system, then our measure of success cannot be delivered to us. No matter how hard we try, we will not feel honored. When we strive for validation within a structure fundamentally incapable of providing the recognition we require, we cast our lines into an abyss hoping to fish out acknowledgement and praise. The abyss has no qualms about taking our energy. It drains us without giving back, without returning what we offer in kind. Without filling our cup. And we can only travel so far without a refuel.

The wrong reward system also means we're missing encouraging counterparts and a supportive community of like-minds. Without those, *nothing* we do will ever be good enough. Nothing will satisfy those whom we are trying to please. We will forever be unfulfilled, drained, disappointed. If we remain misaligned, we compromise ourselves. We'll settle for less than we deserve, or worse, feel we don't merit more. And thus our self-worth diminishes.

Eventually we'll be beaten down to the point of betraying our own nature. We'll feel unmotivated. Purposeless. Rudderless. Everything becomes pointless since nothing we do makes the grade. Why care at all?

That's when life grows perilous, our position precarious. When our purpose could perish — and us along with it. We need to make a big change, fast. We need to realign ourselves with the proper reward system and the right community or organization of like-minded individuals who will validate our existence, reaffirm our purpose, and offer the gratification we seek.

After working or living in an environment where we've been starved for validation, a change of scenery can make realignment feel effortless. When it happens, we make a bigger impact with our work; we receive praise, gratitude, appreciation; greater health; spiritual and creative fulfillment; financial gains. And our like-minded company, community, organization or environment is pleased to provide it because it *needs* and *values* what we have to offer. It's naturally symbiotic: they've found their missing piece and we've found our slice of a more fulfilling pie.

Shel Silverstein illustrated this truth in *The Missing Piece* where a triangular wedge (that's us) is seeking where it fits in the world. It doesn't know it, but it's looking for its Pie (our like-minded reward system) into which it fits perfectly. Of course, the Pie is also searching for its Missing Piece. Each is seeking the other. Each desires to be whole.

Search inside yourself as you explore the world. Know that you're not questing solo. As Rumi wrote, "what you seek is seeking you." There *is* a Pie out there where your unique and special Piece fits like a generous slice of pumpkin, a healthy slice of apple, or a tender slice of chocolate creme.

Even if you must traverse a desert, dessert awaits!

Truth Serum:
The feeling of success is known unto you and you alone.
*   *   *
Though externally sought, success is an internal triumph.

Stop Making Cents, Start Making Sense

Making "sense" is about moving into a place of the senses. Sensing. Intuiting. Progressing into a feeling-space where a deep intelligence more profound than logic resides. By attuning to the senses of the body — our heart sense or "heart-mind" — we gain access to a universal power of knowing that transcends what our minds alone can perceive.

A "sense state" rather than a "think state" powers our intuitive sense. It guides our Inner Voice, which is the synthesis of *all* our senses. And our Inner Voice is the amalgam of everything we receive and everything we know on all levels — conscious, unconscious, psychic, intuitive, emotional, physical. This is deep knowledge. Knowledge that is available to us at all times. It's always broadcasting, we just need to tune into it. And by training ourselves to do so, we can strengthen the connection, enhance the signal, find it more easily the dial, and crank up the volume on the broadcast. And that's how we start making "sense."

The paradox is that by doing so—by making sense—we enable ourselves to make more cents in a real way. As we've all heard and many have come to experientially understand, money is not quantified happiness, though we try to equate the two: "Make more money so you can be happier." As if each dollar is a unit of happiness that we can earn, bank and garner interest on. One would think we could purchase happiness given our collective rush to make more money, to buy more stuff, to accumulate more things. But happiness cannot be bought. Therefore money cannot enhance it.

The real happiness, the true value of *cents*, comes from responding to the guidance of our *senses*, our Inner Voice. Our senses are attuned to optimize our total happiness, which yields the greatest cents. And reflects what is truly of value. And that's how by making *sense* we can more *cents*. Because our inner sense directs us to the cents that matter. Makes sense, right?

We often evaluate opportunities based on our logic brain telling us what looks good on paper, what seems financially shrewd from an analytical standpoint, when what we could be doing is tuning into our intuition, our Inner Voice, and allowing guidance to come from within, from a deeper place, from the wellspring of knowledge into which our intuition taps. A part of our it knows the future, a part of it is aware of the infinite unknowable. It measures opportunities based on factors our analytical mind is incapable of figuring into its evaluative calculus. Our logic brain makes thought-*full* decisions informed by what it thinks will be our best chance at earning our living. But when we attune to the feeling and intuitive part of ourselves rather than acquiescing to logic, we actually make more cents. Intuitive cents. Happy cents. The cents that matter.

Ironically, by stopping our inclination to make cents, our decisions make better sense and create greater value for everyone involved. Following our intuition invites *our most enhanced version of life and well-being coupled with our maximum contribution to the world*. Which is another great way to define success.

Our Inner Voice is plugged into cosmic knowing. And while we might feel reassured by making decisions based on what pencils out correctly, our formulaic analysis is only useful when it reinforces our gut feeling. Even if our brainy calculations disprove our Inner Voice's intuition, we should go with our gut *over* our head, not the other way around.

Analytics cannot override Inner Voice. Our Inner Voice has a lot more information at its disposal: It knows everything our subconscious does, it knows the future and the past, it knows how things are going to develop and unfold within the infinite organizing power of the Universe because it is plugged into Cosmic Consciousness. It knows what synchronicities lay in store and which pies are missing a slice that only our missing piece can fill.

Tapping into our Inner Voice is like seeing a blockbuster while wearing 3D glasses at an IMAX theater. We are getting the biggest, fullest, clearest, most immersive picture imaginable. Evaluating life with our logical, analytical mind is like looking at that giant IMAX screen through a monocular viewfinder where we only get to observe a tiny portion of the theater. We might find ourselves watching the glowing green exit sign above the door, for example, or the red velvet curtain, or the back of the person's head in front of us, or even a small corner of the action taking place onscreen. It's not that one's logic brain isn't seeing clearly, it's just perceiving a sliver of the big picture.

If our decision-making ignores the rest of the 3D IMAX motion picture experience, then it's as if we're viewing life through a narrow window. With blinders on. So don't shrink your vision to...

that

when you can have

THIS!

Truth Serum:
Our inner sense directs us to the cents that matter.

Ample

Ample is a higher standard, a better benchmark than *more*.

How much is "ample?" Ample is one's needs being met *and then some*. Ample is just enough and then *a bit* more. Ample is plentiful, abundant, robust. Ample is not profligate nor greedy. It's not limitless nor inexhaustible. It's not bottomless, ceaseless, all-you-can-eat. It's not take-as-much-as-you-can-get. It's comfortable, healthy, sated satisfaction. And maybe a bit *extra*.

These days, ingratitude seems trendy while gratitude is in short supply. And though it might be easier to jump on the bandwagon of ungraciousness, if what you have is ample then be grateful because ample is the better example.

If greed were good, ample would be gold. Because ample is enough. And enough *is* enough. It's a generous helping. A full plate. And dessert. Any more than that and you're bloating yourself, ingesting more than is healthy. More than your share. And the excuse that just because you can, you should, is a fallacy.

When you do, you're adding girth to your waistline. Packing on excess for use when resources are scarce, say, in those winter months. But global temps are rising. Winter is short. And you don't fast even though you could (and probably should). Greater girth requires more calories to sustain it. Eventually all-you-can-eat isn't even enough.

More breeds *more*. Like coins for your coffers saved for the rainy day that never comes. Larger coffers require more spoils to fill them. And thus, the insatiable cycle of more overtakes us. The more we have the more we *need*. And the less satisfaction we draw from each additional increment.

Gandhi recognized the world has enough "for everyone's need, but not everyone's greed." So let's shoot for *ample* as the new "more." *Ample* meets our need because *more* won't sate our greed.

And then, when you've had enough, when you are filled to satiety, there's even a tad extra. A dollop bonus. A cherry for the top of your ample pudding.

Truth Serum:
Let ample meet your need because more won't
sate your greed. Ample is the better example.

Closed for Busyness

There is a distinction between having a day that is *full* and a day that is *busy*.

Busy is empty calories.

Busy is an hour (or two) evaporating on Facebook.

Busy is a hundred emails in your inbox hanging over your head, weighing on your mind.

Busy is unsatisfying, diffusive and chaotic.

Busy is trite, prosaic, hackneyed: a cliché of such whopping magnitude that "busy" has become meaningless. To utter the word is to say nothing at all. To say one is "busy" is to waste one's breath. And the time to speak it.

These days "busy" is a given. A standard. It goes without saying. It's unnecessary. Irrelevant. Irreconcilable. I resolve to strike busy from my own vocabulary and I suggest you do the same.

"How are you?"

"Busy."

Let's try that again. "How are you?"

"Ah... overwhelmed, fulfilled, grateful, intrigued, bored, empty, energized, excellent, enervated, up, down, sideways..."

Reply with something *meaningful* rather than *meaningless*. We're ALL busy. Very busy. Too busy. Too busy to bother. When we announce we're "busy," we signal to others: "I don't have time for you. You're keeping me from all the important things keeping me busy."

"Busy" is a reply that says, "Don't ask anything of me because I don't have the space for it." Busy tells others, "You're not important enough for me to prioritize."

But what if someone was calling to offer you tickets to the New York Knicks? Or to Coachella? Or to invite you waterskiing in Bimini? Or to the Oscars? Or to Paris for the weekend?

You're reply of "Busy!" to "How are you?" is an immediate slap in the face of the inviter. If you're so "busy," how will you have time for an appealing invitation? You'd be giving something up. You're telling the person that whatever they might offer must compete with all your important business.

In effect, when you say, "I'm busy," you're not open for *business*. You're closed for *busyness*.

But we can always make room for something that fulfills us. Even when we're at capacity, even though we're stuffed to the brink. As with dessert, there's always room for something sweet. Miraculously, we can make room for sugar.

What's the sugar of your life? Are you ever too replete for laughs, pleasure, love? Are you ever too full for fun?

Have you ever left a weekend get-together and complained: "That was *too* pleasurable! I laughed *too* hard. I *never* want to do that again." Have you ever seen a movie that was "too entertaining?" Have you ever been on a date so perfectly romantic that you regretted making time for it?

We're so busy being "busy" that we forget the reason we're so busy to begin with: to be fulfilled, to be happy, to be in joy, to be and to feel successful.

Instead we use "busy" as a badge of honor. Busy is the cross we bear. Busy is our excuse for everything: for not showing up, for not making the grade, for being tired, stressed, distracted… Busy is a taskmaster. Busy is obligatory. Busy is cruise control, autopilot, being asleep at the wheel. Busy doesn't sound like fun. Which begs the question: Are the people claiming to be busy getting any…? Fun, that is?

Busy is boring. Busy is rote. Busy is routine. And who wants to be in the same state as everyone else?

Everyone is busy! Kids are busy. Grandparents and great-grandparents are busy. Students are busy. Teachers are busy. Doctors and nurses and lawyers and engineers and scientists and politicians and professors and consultants and full-time moms and authors and newscasters and your accountant and your boss and your employees and your niece and your aunt and your father in-law and your fifth-grader... They're all busy. And so are you.

You. Are. Just. Like. Everyone. Else.

If that suits your program and satisfies your spirit, then stick to it. If the shoe fits, wear it. But if you prefer to act your age and not your shoe size, then maybe you can do the twirl with another expression that suits your druthers (whatever druthers are).

Here's a suggestion: Instead of busy, try "full" on for size. "Full" is more accurate. More descriptive. More meaningful. And seldom used. While "busy" is empty calories—consuming a bag chips that leaves you unsatisfied—"full" is healthy satisfaction. Full cures your cravings. Full slakes your thirst. Full stands at the heart of being fulfilled.

So get full, be full, live fully. Strike "busy" from your vocabulary so the next time you're asked, you can respond with your whole self.

"How's life?"

"Full."

Ahh, that's more like it. Not "busy." *Full.*

You're complete, but still have room for something sweet.

Truth Serum:
Don't get "busy," strive for "full." Full is complete,
but still leaves room for something sweet.

73

The Ambition of Light

"Have light. Will travel."

Light will travel. And travel light. Help it along: reflect it, project it, usher it in, receive it, don't impede it. Speed the plow even though light doesn't need our help to expedite its progress — it travels at light speed! And it goes everywhere it can. Finds every crevice, every nook and cranny. It's an equal opportunity illuminator.

Light is the universe's ground state. The best way to augment it is not to block it, lock it up, shut it out or shield ourselves from it. Light wants to be everywhere.

Allowing light to pass through us unimpeded makes us translucent. But we can also amplify it. Magnify it. Radiate and harness it. When we act as facets. Like that of a diamond. The more facets we possess, the more faces to catch the light, the more "fire" in our stone.

Light abounds in infinite supply. It's a limitless resource of the cosmos. As luminous beings, we can be fonts that radiate our own light. When we are open and receptive to where light shines. When we receive it. And reflect it and direct it toward others.

Because that's the ambition of light. To radiate and illuminate, warm and comfort, grow and inspire. To go wherever it can. To de-void the void. To bring the love. To draw us into its radiance. To fill the spaces into which it is invited.

So invite the light. In so doing you will amplify the brilliance within you. The human heart is a lustrous prism. The more light you allow, the more you are filled, the more luminous you become. And radiant beings can't help but to spill their light into the cup of another.

So luxuriate in the warmth of light. Bathe in its life-giving gleam. Throw open the curtains, raise the blinds. Do nothing more than allow yourself to bask in its pervasive nature. Hold out your cup. It can fill volumes.

Because the ambition of light is to spread itself. Like love, light wants to reach all creatures, penetrate all of Creation.

Light, like love, is boundless.

Light, like love, transforms the darkness.

Light is love. And love, light.

They are equally ambitious wavelengths.

And light's ambition knows no bounds.

Truth Serum:
The more light you allow, the more luminous you become.

| SPIRIT |

What is good for you is God for you.

~ Truth

Spiritual Legacy

What is your Spiritual Legacy?

You have a familial legacy. An academic and professional legacy. Perhaps a wealth legacy. A wisdom legacy. A creative legacy. Maybe even an athletic, aesthetic and genetic legacy. But what is your *spiritual* legacy?

Your Spiritual Legacy is the legacy that ties to purpose. It is *the* theme of your life. Theme is what endures. Ideas may prevail in the short run. Concepts might reel you in. Premises may sell. But knowing the theme imbued in your work, in your being, is the key to greatness and longevity. It's how the dots connect. It's what binds you to others. Theme is synchronous, harmonious and synonymous with purpose.

Theme is the current that runs through your life. Theme is what persists. Theme is the pH test. The can-we-make-a-hundred-episodes-from-this-show test. The career longevity test. Theme communicates to others that you know what your story is REALLY about. What your LIFE is really about. What YOU are really about.

You likely won't start there. You'll start with what's on the surface: premise, plot, even character. The illusions that play upon the screen. But what's hidden? What's behind the screen and beyond it? Those are the larger truths. The self-evident ones. The subconscious, unconscious, and super-conscious ones tied to universal truths.

Spirit is what endures. Spirit is the soul, literally, of who you are. It is you at the deepest level. And who is that? You are the only one who can define that. It is the you *behind* the you that you identify *as* you. It is the one, as the yogis say, who asks the question. It is the *unconditioned* mind, the inner self, the greater self. Which is why it is so important to "know thyself." And why that is the holy axiom of all spiritual

78

teachings. Knowing thyself speaks to purpose. Knowing thyself speaks to meaning. Speaks to destiny. To calling. To the legacy of Spirit within. Hence, Spiritual Legacy.

To align with the supremacy of legacy, the first requirement is to identify your purpose. The second is to adjust your life to comport with that purpose, with who you are, to live that truth. The third is to ensure that the choices you make and the actions you take are fulfilling the promise of your purpose. Those three elements sum up your Spiritual Legacy.

Spiritual Legacy is why you were put on this earth. It's why you chose to come here (because you *did* choose). It's the wake you will leave behind when you're gone. Your spirit leaves an imprint, an echo, a vibrational reverberation and perhaps a path for others to follow or shoulders upon which to stand. Spiritual Legacy is the resonant image by which others remember you. It's what gives you staying power.

Mighty legacies are the result of potent, universal, humanitarian themes. The notion of leaving the world better off for your presence in it is a mark of Spiritual Legacy.

What will be *your* legacy? What do you desire it to be? Let that guide your choices from this day forward. Choices for yourself. In your interactions with others. In your pursuits and endeavors. The more love you weave, the further your legacy shall prevail. To echo Gandhi, a being of great Spiritual Legacy, when choosing a course of action, always choose the path that leads to greater love. *Love is the catalyst of legacy.*

How we behave will be reinforced by how we perceive the behavior of others. The way we act is reflected back to us by the actions of others. Our deeds are based on our fundamental expectation of the world. So act in word and deed in ways that inspire others to act similarly. Reflectively.

Indeed, if we trust others, working from a place of trust, then we will be shown trust in return. As Hemingway wrote, "The way to make people trustworthy is to trust them." If we don't trust others, then that will be reflected in their distrust of *us.* Thus we shall distrust and in turn be distrusted.

As we seek, so shall we find. So seek for greater riches that you wish to bequeath the world. Search for betrayal, we'll find treachery and we shall betray. Seek compassion, we'll find empathic kindness and we shall embrace our fellow travelers. Seek love, we'll find humanity's greatest treasure and we shall grow a loving bounty.

Spiritual Legacy is bigger than any one act or accomplishment. It is the culmination of all the tiny, individual acts and cumulative achievements of our lives. It is the spiritual intention behind our experiential direction.

Spiritual Legacy is our soul's expression and therefore the Divine expression of who we are. When acting in harmony with Spiritual Legacy, we are acting in concert with Spirit, in union with the Universe, in collaboration with the Divine. Getting in tune with our Spiritual Legacy puts us in contact with our Divine purpose and brings us closer to Creation. As we seek to promote and further our Spiritual Legacy, we find guidance and serendipity and synchronicity along our path because we are doing our soul's work, our Spirit's work, which is really God's work.

With clear intention we sew our Spiritual Legacy. With each action we add another stitch. In the effort, we weave the threads that color and bind the very fabric of humanity.

Truth Serum:
Spiritual Legacy is the human reflection
of the cosmic connection
behind the spiritual intention
of our experiential direction.

Begging Bowls for Spirit

We are begging bowls for Spirit. If we just get out of the way, open ourselves, and empty ourselves to allow Spirit to come in, to fill us, to guide us, we can have it all. Everything we want. Everything we need. All that we desire.

Our primary challenge in this life, our task if you will—our purpose—is to get out of the way and let Spirit move through us, inhabit us, dance with us, flow around us. And when we learn to flow with it, life can be effortless, joyful, worry-free and painless.

The force of Spirit can deliver us from evil, but it's more inclined to deliver us to joy. The effort applied from our end is that of allowing. Like opening the door and inviting Spirit to step across the threshold and enter our dwelling.

We offer our open bowl to the universe and ask that it be filled with Spirit. Spirit as our source of strength. Spirit as our guide. Spirit as our guardian.

We are but beggars. For to live without Spirit is an impoverished existence even if one has much on the material plane and many matters to attend to. All of our accumulated "matter," matters not in the grand scheme of All That Is.

When the realization comes—and it will—that grandiose material possessions and ambitious yearnings provide no lasting solace for they are bereft of meaning, we will find ourselves begging for fulfillment, thirsting for the elixir that will slake our soul's unquenchable thirst. We will find ourselves beggars. Holding out our gilded bowl, imploring someone or something to fill it.

Whether prince or pauper, we are begging bowls for Spirit. For it is Spirit alone that can slake our thirst. Spirit unaided that can fill our bellies. Spirit by itself that can satiate us. If we allow it to do its work. To serve its purpose.

Offer your begging bowl to the unknown. Invite Spirit to fill it. Perhaps it will answer; will offer you ladlefuls. Will warm you and comfort you and satisfy your hunger. And you shall find a place among the humble beggars who lie not along the gutters of the citadels, but occupy the palaces of kings.

Truth Serum:
Spirit can deliver us from evil,
but it's more inclined to deliver us to joy.

Triumph of the Human Spirit

When we are inspired by a story that showcases triumph over hardship, or healing over sickness, or victory over defeat, we say the story is a triumph of the *human spirit*.

It's not the individual on their own who accomplishes the thing, who overcomes or endures, but something bigger, something internal, something transcendent, something eternal. That's spirit. Spirit *within* us. And connected to spirit writ large. A triumph of spirit is a triumph with a capital "S." A triumph for all spirits everywhere.

When a triumphant being's singular story is told, it raises spirits like a rising tide raises all vessels. When we see that one person can do it, we know that we all can. When we witness greatness in one of us, we realize there's greatness in all of us. Our own greatness. Waiting to be revealed.

The four-minute mile. Breaking the sound barrier. Solo circumnavigation of the globe via aircraft or watercraft. Summiting Everest without oxygen. Healing from cancer without radiation. Patience in incarceration. Leadership despite starvation. Peace in the face of aggression. Love despite oppression. From handicapped to superhero. From blind to sighted. Fame and fortune for art once derided. Sending humanity to space, to the Moon, to Mars, to the stars....

Impossible. Until it is not.

Impossible. Until we see.

Impossible. Until a triumph.

A triumph of the human spirit.

Credit goes to the human. But the human was not alone. Spirit is the uncredited party. Spirit got it done. Spirit is the universal unseen. God. The Creator. Source. Working through us, within us, manifesting itself on our plane of existence.

In Spirit, humanity succeeds.

In Spirit, it shall be done.
In Spirit, all things are possible.
Because Spirit… is responsible.
And it doesn't even ask for top billing.

Truth Serum:
A triumph for one spirit is a triumph for all.
Anything is possible when Spirit is responsible.

CONFLICT & COMMUNICATION

Our best learning often comes from our worst experiences.

~ Truth

Universal Solvent

The Universe simultaneously hands us conflicts and the means to their solution. Every puzzle comes with a set of instructions and the elements required to piece it together. If a conflict didn't have a solution what would be the point? You would abandon the puzzle. "This doesn't fit together," one might say. "It's pointless," and then walk away.

Life doesn't want you to walk away from it. It wants you to *engage* it. The Cosmos, the Universe, Loving Consciousness, is always unfolding and ever-burgeoning infinitely outward in a desire to know itself, to expand its own awareness, playfully, mysteriously, adventurously. It doesn't create problems without simultaneously holding the key—and the means—for their solution. The Universe is its *own* universal solvent.

We just have to do our part. Take the case. Roll up our sleeves. Follow the breadcrumbs. Puzzle the pieces. Engage our own faculties which engages the abundant faculties of the Cosmos.

By challenging us, the Universe is perpetually challenging its own creativity. It is asking, just as the philosophers and thinkers, artists and tinkerers, lovers and leaders, doers and be-ers of all ages have been asking, "How can I do better? Create grander? Love greater?"

The Universe *is* thinking what you're thinking.

Truth Serum:
The Universe simultaneously hands us conflicts
and the means to their solution.

Words Are Spells

We can become witness to and keenly aware of the magic at play in our own lives. With a little practice, we can harness the power and intelligence of a thoughtful and responsive Universe. When we honor our magical experiences, we attune to the magic of existence.

Words are spells, after all. They conjure the outcomes we describe and powerfully usher in the things we write down or articulate aloud. Putting thoughts into words is a powerful step toward manifesting the results we seek because words are the symbolic representation of our imaginings, desires, yearnings. They are the crystallization of the images in our mind, the feelings in our hearts, the encapsulation of our dreams.

Words can also be a vehicle for discarding the negative thoughts that hold us in their grip. A useful tool to release that which obsesses us is to show up on the page, to write an email, to compose a letter, to journal about all the ruminant swirlings in our minds—or hearts—about a person or subject. In so doing, we can alleviate the strain of those thoughts on our psyche, clearing it for more useful musings, while simultaneously sending the message into the Universe for the other person to perceive — subliminally, subconsciously, tacitly.

Even if our email remains unsent or our letter un-mailed, or our journaled thoughts unread by another, our appeal is often, if not always, heard by its intended recipient. Incredibly, the efficacy of our missive is the same as having sent it! Like magic.

Even if they don't respond directly, they may later admit that they thought of us, that they regret what happened between us, that they felt compelled to reach out to us. By inscribing our thoughts on the Universe, the cosmos ensures those thoughts are delivered — with 100% reliability! The intended recipient might apologize, they might make amends or they might simply alter their behavior. Rest assured, there will be some response from Creation as the Universe is responsive to our inquiries, requests and articulations. It desires that we resolve our differences, heal our wounds, mend our fences, grow ourselves and our relationships.

In this way, words *are* spells. As magical beings all we must do is fill the page before us with the enchantments we wish to cast and then conjure the magic all around us by inscribing them on the parchment of the cosmos.

Truth Serum:
Words are spells by which we conjure the magic
that frolics omnipresent at our fingertips.

Styrofoam Wind Chimes

Quiet. Do you hear that? That's the sound of styrofoam wind chimes swinging in the breeze. If you listen carefully you'll hear... *nothing*. Because styrofoam doesn't chime.

Hanging styrofoam wind chimes is like harboring an intent without crystalizing it through vocalization. We must cast our spells—spells of manifestation, reconciliation, intention, connection—by speaking our words.

In Latin, viva voce (pronounced "vee-vah vo-chay") is literally "living voice." Our voices *are* alive. They evince the life within us by expressing the unique notes of the human instrument. How effective would the conjurer be with a wave of her hand, but no spells to speak?

Speaking of spells... remember the Speak N Spell? Even though it was a child's electronic plaything it wasn't just a spell toy. Words were spoken. They were verbalized first by a me-ch-an-i-cal doodad. Then the child typed the word. The voice spoke. The message was understood. Its meaning received. Then the word manifested as form on an LED.

It doesn't matter if our sounds are mechanical or animal. Grunt or growl. Japanese or Italian. Latin or French. Russian or Mandarin. Tagalog or Thai. Words are symbols that give shape to the hopes, dreams, intentions and expressions that don't yet have form. When those words are whispered or declared, hummed or sung, hooted or hollered, it magnifies their power manifold.

So speak your spell. Fortify your request with the linguistic potency of sound. Utter your dreams aloud to usher them inbound.

What bold appeal can we make of the Universe if we're putting it out there without wanting anyone, including ourselves, to hear it?

Truth Serum:
Give your words the vehicle of voice
to conjure the magic of manifestation.
*   *   *
Utter your dreams aloud to usher them inbound.

Connection Intention

The *intention* we bring to the party is the party favor we intend to leave with. When in doubt, bring a connection intention. It's foolproof.

Holding a connection intention is like baby-proofing your house: it allows exploration without any harm done. You are free to roam without fear of poking an electrical socket.

Nothing negative results from connection. Even *disconnection* tells you something. It tells you what you need to know: to try something different; try somebody different; to find another way.

Seeking connection is asking to be hooked up energetically with your tribe. Whether it's an individual or a group, human or animal, spiritual or intellectual, psychic or physical. It's a quest for counterparts. Confederates. Community.

Intention for connection is a spiritual yearning. It comes from a deep place within because it's through connection that we enter a sacrosanct realm. A place that feels secure. Like home. Where we can be ourselves with others *like* ourselves. It's why when we feel connection time stops. We're in tune. We feel Oneness. Our experience of separateness ends. It's a cherished feeling. An exultant sensation. A transcendent state of being.

The Universe is infinitely abundant. There are like-minded bedfellows among us, around us. We have only to ask, to seek them out, to set our intention to find them.

Connection Intention.

The phrase plays upon the palate. And fills our plate. It's how we know that there are others who share the journey with us. Other beings who recognize us—*really* see us—because we recognize them. Their truths are our own. And that's how we know we are not alone. Even if we feel as though we are.

Wish to connect? Ask with intent and ye shall receive. Just like you, the cosmos conspires to commune.

Connection Intention.

It makes the soirée worthwhile. Especially when you leave the party with a favor you *really* can take home with you.

Truth Serum:
Intend to connect, yearn to attune.
Just like you, Creation conspires to commune.

Know Better

"I know better." Every hear this? Ever say this? The implication is that *I* know better than *you*. It's a frustrating declaration to hear. And to make.

The truth is that you may know better. In fact, you *do* know better. But only where one person is concerned. You know better for *you*. And even that's just a... maybe.

The Universe is the only entity that knows best. You *think* you know better. But it's only when you're plugged into Universal knowing that you actually know better. There's always room for surprises. The more certain we know something — the outcome of an election, for example, or that we've covered all of our bases, or that an intended result is a sure-fire "lock" — the more likely the cosmos is to surprise us with all the things we didn't know that we thought we did.

To admonish someone—like a child—with the pronouncement "I know better" is really just to say that you *think* you know better based on past experience and that your experience has taught *you* a lesson. But that you know better for another is fallacy. You can't know better for anyone but yourself. Each of us has our own path, our own journey, our own guidance system, our own life lessons to learn.

So don't deny another's lesson. It's like slipping someone the answers during a test: they might get the answers right, but they don't know *why* they're right. They haven't learned anything except that someone else had the answer. And even guesswork—a shot in the dark—is preferable to being handed the "right" answer because a best guess taps intuition, fate and grand design.

Often the *wrong* answer yields a positive learning experience. Isn't it true that the answers we missed, the questions we got wrong, the word we misspelled, the knowledge we lacked are the things we *really* learn and retain?

If there is truly a desire to get something "right," to prove our prowess, to own the material, well, those are the lessons we remember forever. It's the word we'll never misspell again (two "L's" *and* two "N's" in "millennium"), the factoid we'll never forget (America is named for Amerigo Vespucci), the knowledge we'll retain until the day we die (ontogeny recapitulates phylogeny).

And that's because we were "incorrect of our own accord." It was our mistake to make and we made it. And now we own it. We got the answer "wrong," the points were deducted, our test score suffered, our GPA took a hit. But if we cared to find out why, to inquire about the right answer, to amend our work, to solve the problem correctly... then the lesson stays with us for the rest of our days. Much more than the things we didn't miss. Because those are the things we already knew. We had those in the bag.

Like so much in life, the painful sweeping red marks we receive on our tests, that bright blotch on our essay, the lashes on our bodies, the scars on our psyches, the wounds to our hearts are the lessons from which we learn the most. They hurt, they're painful — physically, intellectually, emotionally, spiritually — but they prompt the most growth, the most insight, the biggest "Ah-hahs," the most resounding and resilient learning.

So whether you're a teacher now or ever desire to be or or never thought you were, if you think you "know better," know that you don't know better for anyone but yourself.

If you really know better, know it's better to allow someone to learn their own lesson, to follow their own guidance, to let them think they know better whether they do or they don't.

If you know better you'll know that the easy way is not as effective an heuristic (learning) tool as the hard way.

If you really know better then you'll know that allowing another to know better is the better bet.

Truth Serum:
If you knew better then you'd know better
than to "know better."

Compassion

Compassion is passionate empathy for another being. More than understanding or feeling bad for someone or their situation or hardship, compassion requires a fervor, an ardor to relate to the perspective and experience of another. It's not "Tsk-tsk, too bad for them." It's not "I feel sorry for you." Compassion is reframing another's experience in the context of one's own life.

This isn't to say it's putting oneself in another's exact same shoes or circumstances. We needn't experience the loss of a loved one, for example, or the stress of a health crisis to express compassion. It's about stepping up to step *outside* oneself to listen without judgment, to meet another being on their level; to feel their sense of loss, happiness, sadness, jealousy, anger, hurt, betrayal, joy, celebration; to be with that emotion; to be with them fully without appraising their suffering or point of view as greater or lesser, better or worse, superficial or tragic, indulgent or severe.

For how is it to truly know the experience of another? It's impossible. The infinite variety of fate, experience and choice that shapes each our lives—an evolving process that continues to mold us on a daily basis!—creates the unique perspective each of us calls our own. It's the membrane through which we experience reality. Our unique worldview.

It's inaccurate to say that we can know the experience or feelings of someone else. But we can try. With enthusiasm, effort and alacrity. With passion—energy, vitality, eagerness, acceptance—we can connect with another. Connecting heartfully. Intuiting emotionally. Communing enthusiastically. All of which equals *compassion*.

When you show compassion for another, you bring *passion* to the party. Passion isn't passive. Passion doesn't just sit there. Passion presupposes active engagement. And it's not only a word to describe arousal. Though passion does arouse something: it stokes a palpable fervor within. Compassion is a *passionate* fervor to connect. Compassion means getting passionate about the act of listening, connecting and relating to the person whom you are showing compassion.

If you can't bring that much of yourself to the equation, then you're not evincing compassion. You might have sympathy. You might be a shoulder to cry on. But you're not compassionate unless you are a *passionate* presence.

Compassion requires commitment. You have to choose to step into it in order to step up for another.

Truth Serum:
Compassion is reframing another's experience in
the context of one's own life.

Wild & Precious

"Your one wild and precious life"† is sacred. Protect it with everything you've got.

If one does not foster the circumstances that encourage honor and respect from others, then one is encouraging circumstances that will allow for diminishment, disparagement and disregard of oneself.

Old habits die hard. Allowing mistreatment to become a habit makes it more and more difficult to break that habitual behavior in another. It also becomes harder to break one's own habit of expecting *less*.

Human beings are pliant. We can get used to anything. But that doesn't mean we should. We must train others to treat us in the manner in which we wish to be treated. Otherwise they will become accustomed to treating us as they desire to do so. Which is usually by default: their set way of being, of doing, of acting in the world. It's their unconscious manner, their autonomic behavior toward others, which is a reflection of their attitude about themselves.

We can elevate our own status by establishing the type of treatment we deserve from others. The first way to do this is to treat ourselves well. We can't honestly and fully honor another unless we know what it feels like to honor *ourselves*, to pamper ourselves, to cater to our own needs, to feel taken care of, to feel dignified and respected.

In setting our own example, we are establishing the blueprint for how we desire to be treated. For how we insist on being treated. Anything less than we deserve should be rejected. Anything that meets our standard should be accepted with grace and gratitude, appreciation and reciprocity.

Trading oneself for another, substituting one's own standards for another's, is a foolhardy endeavor. Suffering at the expense of others—letting others transgress our boundaries—is unhealthy. It should make us angry. Furious. And that ire is a sign our thresholds have been crossed.

If we don't set our own standard, then the standard will be set by someone else! Typically the standard by which they treat themselves. And far too many treat themselves poorly. They feel they don't deserve much so they don't expect much; they don't offer much so therefore don't receive much.

So set your own standard. Raise the bar. Be the example for how others should be treating you and for how others deserve to be treated themselves. No matter how high or low we set our expectations, they are usually met.

Your one life is "wild and precious." Don't allow yourself to be treated by any other benchmark but your own. If you do, it's no one else's fault, it's just their *default*, which is really your own fault.

Truth Serum:
Allowing another to treat us by default is our own fault.

† From *"The Summer Day"* by Mary Oliver.

Integrity Is a Mutuality

Integrity is when what we think, what we say and what we do are in alignment. Gandhi also described this as happiness.

When we say someone is "in integrity" or "acting with integrity" what we mean is that they behave and act in alignment with *our own* values. It's when they are true to *us*. To our way of being.

But if personal integrity is when one acts in alignment with one's own values and beliefs, that is, when we are true to *ourselves*, then another's personal integrity guides them to be true to *themselves*.

So there's the rub, you see? If we are in integrity, we are acting in alignment with our *own* principals in the same way that another with integrity acts in alignment with *their* own standards. Virtue and vice are a matter of perspective. If core values—theirs and ours—aren't aligned, then our relationship is fated for failure and we are destined for disappointment.

Whether formal or informal, with each individual with whom we interact we are entering into a relationship contract. That contract has mutually agreed-upon terms of engagement. Both parties agree how they will treat each other and what the exchange of value is between them. Which behaviors are acceptable and which are not. When someone breaches, we know it, we feel it, even if they don't. In same way we might accidentally or unintentionally breach our role. It's only fair if we are made aware of it and discuss how to cure the problem.

It's not enough to declare that someone has "no integrity" when we find another's behavior outrageous, unbelievable or offensive. That behavior, outrageous as it may seem, could be consistent with what they've *always* thought, said and done. From their perspective, they have integrity.

We've all witnessed acts of betrayal where the betraying party is confronted only to be astonished that anyone would find theirs a betraying deed. The clear explanation is that their actions are in line with their own brand of integrity. We just didn't get the memo that betrayal was a brand extension.

This is why our relationship contracts need to be referenced, modified, and amended as our ties evolve. As relationships are anything but stagnant and fixed, our agreements should be organic and alive and subject to periodic review. When we find our boundaries transgressed, when our feelings are hurt, when we witness behavior that clues us in to a potential "Uh-oh" on the horizon, it's preferable to check in with each other before the inevitable shit hits the fan.

So give your dynamic connections the performance review they deserve — and require! Get on the same page, establish clear terms, act consistent with the codicils, tenets and values that are *mutually* understood to govern. Because that's acting with mutual integrity.

And that's why integrity… is a *mutuality*.

Truth Serum:
Integrity is when what we think, what we say
and what we do are in alignment.

PROBLEMS & SOLUTIONS

We can't control life events. All we can control is our response to those events.

~ Truth

God's Handle

God handles a lot. In fact, He handles everything. All of our problems. And their solutions!

We just don't realize this because problems and solutions come to us at different points in our linear perception of time. But, like Morpheus in *The Matrix* offering Neo a red pill in one hand and a blue pill in the other, God offers us a problem in one hand and the solution in the other. Both are offered at the same time. Problem? Problem solved.

We can only grab one at a time. And that's our problem—er, limitation—as human beings. Interestingly, even if we grabbed for the solution, we would then have to take the problem, too, otherwise what would we be solving?

Knowledge, creativity and growth all arrive from our impulse and ability to problem-solve. We are a species obsessed with problems: math problems, word puzzles, physics challenges, engineering quandaries, architectural riddles, organizational hurdles, political dilemmas, natural disasters, media mishaps... Problem solving is how we evolved.

We need to be confident in our ability to solve our issues, personally and globally, because the same creative dynamism that gave rise to our planet, and to us, has the inherent ability to solve all the problems borne of its own invention and, in turn, human endeavor. In other words, The Creator has a handle on all of Creation.

For as amiss as things may often seem, we can continuously course-correct to set them straight again. For as insurmountable as life issues often feel, God didn't get us this far to drop us on the noggin. Like a good parent, He *wants* to help us. He *wants* to guide us to avoid suffering. He does so through our connection to Spirit through our Inner Voice, our intuition, our Heart-Mind. But like any parent knows who has attempted to protect their children from pain and disappointment, sometimes our kids just can't be spared the lesson despite our best efforts. Often, for children to learn what needs to be learned, they must experience the lesson themselves — unmitigated, unfiltered, unadulterated. We may call it the "hard way," but occasionally, it's the *only* way.

Parenting children is like God parenting us: He *wants* to spare us the painful parables, the agonizing allegories, the testing trials. He attempts to do so through Divine guidance. By steering us clear of misfortune. By directing us in all possible ways through the power of the cosmos. But, like children, we surmise that we "know better" despite the messages coming through to us. We deny our inner knowing, our inner truth. A part of us chooses the harsh lesson, the problematic predicament, the consequences of the "hard way" despite all intuitive evidence to the contrary. Like the child who *must* touch the hot stove, the sharp blade or the fragile crystal we expressly told them *not* to touch, we're simply "asking for it."

And who is God—who are we as parents—to deny children the lessons they most profoundly desire to learn on their own? Painful as it is to watch them make the mistakes we wanted to spare them, there is a lesson in it for us: We cannot deny another's learning though we may try.

As with any instruction, first God whispers to us, lovingly urging an alternate choice. If we don't listen, He taps us on the shoulder. No dice? We'll get a shove sideways, backwards or forwards to get our attention. If that doesn't do the trick—if we *still* refute the message—prepare for a cosmic two-by-four. The clobber is gonna hurt. It *will* leave a mark. But the wallop gets us back on track. Whether we like the manner of the adjustment or not.

Hey, we were *asking* for it. Wouldn't it have been better to listen when He's whispering softly in our ear or tapping us gently on the shoulder? It's up to us whether we receive a pat on the back or kick in the head. Both serve the same purpose. To help. To guide. To instruct.

Whether tough love or gentle caress, God's got us covered. He's the ultimate challenge-deliverer and problem-solver. He has a hand in everything, for they are mighty hands. And you know what they say about big hands....

Big handle.

Truth Serum:
God offers us problems and solutions simultaneously.
We can't grasp them both at once. But He can.

Dis-Illusion

When we feel disillusioned by life circumstances, it's our Inner Voice, our intuitive self, piercing the veil of "reality."

*Dis*illusion is the recognition that the current *illusion* we are subscribed to no longer works. The "dis-" is our deeper selves' rejection of what no longer serves our—nor the collective—greater good.

According to Einstein, "Reality is merely an illusion, albeit a very persistent one." This persistence feels "real" because we all agree to believe in it. When a periodic sense of disillusionment washes over us, it's our unconscious awareness of the mirage. It's our intuition speaking up: "Wait a minute. I'm not digging on the current state of my reality."

Our life experience is our co-creation with the Universe, a product of our choices, our habits, our attitude, our values, which become our destiny. We can co-create an alternative experience by making different choices, forming new habits, shifting our attitude, adjusting our values, ergo altering our destiny.

Disillusion is a handy blade to pierce the veil, thus revealing the "illusion" for what it is. It allows us a peek behind the curtain to empower our choice of fresh adventure: new experiences that usher their way toward us as we take faithful steps toward them.

So if you find your beliefs blown, your convictions crumbled, your visions vivisected, give it a name. Feeling disappointed, disheartened or discontented could be *disillusion.* If so, see it as a positive—and essential—first step toward improvement. Disillusion, while arising from feeling *bad,* is a necessary step toward feeling *good.* That is its purpose.

Disillusion is a precursor to finding our way. Disillusion is fuel to blazing new trails. Disillusion helps right what's wrong.

Do not discard disillusion. Discard the things that give rise to it. Disillusion helps you to identify and cast off your old illusions in favor of newfangled ones; to discard illusory ways of being in favor of one's best ways of being.

Disillusion indicates a new life awaits.

Truth Serum:
Don't be disillusioned by disillusion.
Diss your current illusion in favor of a better one.

Know You Don't

Certainty. Certitude. A sense of knowing. We all want it. We all strive for it. We want to be "right," to feel correct. To act with assuredness. To know what we're doing, to know where we're headed, to know the answer. And, yet, sometimes... we just don't know.

And when we don't know, our only comfort in knowing is to *know* we don't know. In other words, we need to own the fact that we don't know. At least, not yet. Despite best efforts, we're stumped. We're not sure which way to head, which end is up. We can feel—we can be—lost.

Acknowledging this is a big step in the right direction when any direction will do. We know we're lost so we seek assistance. We dig out our maps, consult our GPS, pull out our devices to navigate the way. But even though our compass points north, it points to *magnetic north*; perhaps not our *true* north.

So a map, a compass, the North Star, a guiding light... these are just navigation tools. Indicators. We need to find the way ourselves. And that takes time. Takes searching. Takes heading down errant paths and circling back to where we started to venture forth again.

And that's why we need to know when we don't know. When we don't know, we're shrugging our shoulders in a gesture to the cosmos to fill in the blanks, to drop a few breadcrumbs, to chart a heading.

Sometimes when we don't know, it's the only thing we *do* know. But that can be reassuring. If we have certainty about our feeling that we just don't know that *is* something to know.

So know that you *know* you don't know. Own it. Because when you do, it'll set the Universe on a course of delivering possibilities that will teach you what there *is* to know, reaffirm what you *do* know, illuminate what you *can* know, so that you *will* know.

Because sometimes you just don't know, you know?

Truth Serum:
Sometimes the only thing you know is that
you don't know — and that is something to know.
Knowing you don't know will guide you to what you
do know so that you can know, you know?

When Something's Fucked

When something's fucked. And we recognize it as fucked. And we declare it as fucked. Then it *is* fucked.

But "fucked" is a biological imperative. Fucked is the process of creation. Fucked is the path to pregnancy. And to birth. Or rebirth. So in recognizing something being fucked is the potential for something new, something transformed, something being born. Fucked is the genesis, the impetus for conception and creation, for the birth ideas and beings.

Shiva is both Creator *and* Destroyer. The Phoenix rises from the ashes then bursts into flame, crumbling to cinders in order to rise anew. Destruction is a creative act because something *razed* sows the seeds of something *raised*. Like raising a citadel from ruin. Raising a family after an affliction. Or raising oneself in the slipstream of setback.

We conceive new ideas, nurture new concepts, cultivate new awareness, grow new solutions to solve old problems, tired notions, fucked situations.

Sometimes you just have to say "Fuck." Call it out, speak its name, trumpet the truth. When something's fucked, name it. When something's fucked, declare it. When something's fucked, own it. "This... is fucked!"

Because "fuck" is an exclamation that accompanies or describes or leads to a pathway to making love. To union. To two pieces coming together, attempting to be whole.

And that's something everyone needs. And anyone can get excited about.

Truth Serum:
When something's fucked, it's fucked.

This Couldn't Have Come at a Worse Time

When challenge comes at the most inopportune moment we exclaim: "Crap! This couldn't have come at a worse time!"

Any additional problem is unwelcome when we're already overwhelmed. *One more thing* adds insult to injury. Prompts exasperation. Calls inordinate attention to itself.

When we feel the Universe's timing is off, or that we have too much going on, that our plates are overfull and that we're caught in a swirling whirlwind, adding another log to the blaze we're battling elicits the feeling "This is the *worst* thing that could happen right now."

Or is it?

What if the *opposite* were true? What if the very reason for "bad" timing was to re-focus our priorities on what's important, what's imperative, what requires our attention most?

From this perspective, the *worst time* is perhaps the *best time* for something to come. Perhaps the darn thing piles on just as we are getting settled, or as we are at long-last coming to rest, finally catching our breath, recovering our health, landing back on our feet, climbing out of debt or completing some long-term ambition like graduating, starting a new job, moving into our first home, having our first child, finalizing our travel plans... and now *this*? Really? This!?

Yes, THIS!

"It couldn't have come at a worse time" might just be the *best* time. If we flip the script, turn the situation on its ear and gaze upon it from a different perspective. The proverbial straw that broke the camel's back might turn out not to be straw, but spun gold.

That natural disaster? That setback at work? That death in the family? That crisis at school? That financial roadblock? That tsunami of bad news? That *actual* tsunami?

It was the worst of times, it was the best of times. Events come when they come; they are what they are; and it is what it is. Accept it, embrace it, deal with it.

Because it just may augur that the *best* is yet to come.

Truth Serum:
The straw that broke the camel's back
might not be straw at all, but spun gold.

God Is Always Helping

How often in the midst of life's events do we say to ourselves, "This isn't helping!"

We cut our finger while doing dishes and it only adds to the stress we were feeling in the moment.

We misplace our keys while having a tough day.

Our lover is unavailable to listen actively or to provide a needed cuddle.

We get into a fender-bender on the way to an important business meeting. Or a flat tire on the way to pick up our kids.

We get the time wrong for our flight, for the playdate, for the main event.

We suffer a break-up in the midst of some aspect of life breaking down.

We'll, attitude is everything. And rather than reaffirm, "This isn't helping," perhaps we can inquire, "How is this helping?"

Because God is *always* helping. It's all He knows how to do. That's all He does all day, all the time. He helps us. He helps *everything*: grow, learn, evolve, develop, live, love, blossom. *Nothing* that comes from God is unhelpful.

So the next time we catch ourselves asserting, "This isn't helping." Ask for assistance by inquiring "How *does* this help?" And know in your heart that help is on the way. In fact, it's already arrived. Just open yourself to receive it.

And if you need another helping, just ask for one. It's not a single-serving Universe. There's always room for seconds.

Truth Serum:
God is ALWAYS helping.

Let

"Let." Funny word. Short and sweet. Big meaning.

To let: Allow. Permit. Enable. Assent. Relent. Make way.

Letting: Allowing unhindered, unfettered, unobstructed.

Letting go: Releasing. Relinquishing. Unhanding.

There is ease in "letting." It's an exhale, a sigh. Not the holding of breath or gasping for air.

Letting is therapeutic. A palliative elixir of consent.

Ah, to let. Perchance to dream...

Letting is a release, a reduction of stress, a gesture of giving in—not giving up!—and allowing the current to carry us for a stretch.

In tennis, when a ball served hits the top of the net and falls in-bounds, it's called a "let." A let is an allowance. A do-over. A way not to penalize nor favor the server (the giver) nor the receiver. It's a chance to play again.

If *let* feels good, if *let* feels like a needed release or a change of tack or a necessary attitude adjustment, then go ahead and let it into your life.

Let fly. Let loose. Let up.

Let it pass. Let it go. Let it away.

Let it alone. Let it remain. Let it in.

Or simply... let it be.

Truth Serum:
There's power in letting go and letting it be.

HEART-CENTERED LIVING

We must serve our hearts
in order for our hearts to serve us.

Following our heart's intent
leads us to our heart's content.

~ Truth

Where Are You "Hearted?"

Are you racing in the direction your head is telling you or are you traipsing the path your heart has set you on?

As a human race, we're always "headed" somewhere. And typically in a rush to get there. Maybe we should be "hearted" in a more meandering, playful direction. If we tuned into where are our hearts led us, we might be more lovingly-inclined.

Could it be as simple as changing the nomenclature? Could altering the language with which we engage each other prompt a shift from a headspace to a heartspace?

Let's experiment.

If someone is on their way out the door, ask them "Where are you *hearted*?" instead of "Where are you *headed*?"

See if it makes a difference in their countenance or gives them pause. Maybe they'll put a hand to their chest and contemplate for a moment — "Where *am* I hearted?" And that moment's reflection might be enough to alter their course or to reaffirm their intended direction.

How would *you* react if someone asked you, "Where are *you* hearted?" Would you be able to take a moment from where you were headed to divine your heart's intent?

We usually have a set course in mind. Some meeting or appointment to get to, some task to accomplish, some item to cross off our list that requires *heading* out the door, *heading* into traffic, *heading* somewhere to accomplish something. Our eyes narrow and our forehead crinkles in anticipation of getting there, getting it done, getting it off our plates, putting it behind us in order to get onto the *next* thing.

This conditioned existence in which all of us are caught up is heady stuff indeed. Which makes the lives we lead all above the neck. We're perpetually in some kind of head-space. So how can we reorient to heartspace?

Just the thought of "Where am I hearted?" brings the energy of consciousness to the center of our being, into the chest, the ribs, the lungs, the space where we breathe in the ethers of life, where we oxygenate our bodies, where we find *literal* inspiration.

That's why leading from the residence of the heart is an inspired place from which to venture forth. It propels us into the world from the place where our deepest desires and our purest intentions take seed.

When we *think* about where we are hearted, it coerces the mind to contemplate the imperatives of the heart. To acknowledge its vital rhythm.

To ponder "Where am I hearted?" requires us to use our mind's faculties to discern how we honestly feel about the task we're rushing out to do and the intent we hold about it.

So the next time you "head" out the door, take a moment to inquire, *"Where am I hearted?"* Confirm whether your heart desires to venture in your intended direction or if another destination calls. Feel what answer arises within you.

The heart is a feeling instrument, so play it as intended — don't bang away when it requires a gentle strumming. In other words, don't *think* about it, *feel* about it.

"Where are you hearted?" brings you closer to your heart's desire no matter where you are headed.

Truth Serum:
Shift from the domed dwelling of headspace into the open field of heartspace by asking Where Am I Hearted?

120

Head Follows Heart

How could I be so wrong-*headed*?
What was I *thinking*?
I've got to get my *head* in the game!

*   *   *

These are idioms we've heard. Or said. Or experienced. Or observed in others. Or things we've thought, felt or spoken aloud to ourselves. Each expression relates to the where-abouts of our minds with no regard for the vicinity of our *hearts*.

We try to focus by getting our *heads* in the game, or by finding the right *mindset,* or by raising the volume on our *headsets,* but, truly, we're concentrating on the wrong organ. When our minds aren't cooperating, when our focus is fuzzy, when our thoughts are elsewhere, the question we should be asking ourselves is *"Where am I hearted?"*

When the heart connects, the mind respects. It's impossible to have our heart in something and not have our head follow along. It's impossible to engage *heart*fully, but be ab-sent-minded. That's why when our mind is present, but our heart is not, it's a recipe for distraction, for sloth, for acci-dents, for failure. When we are fully, passionately heartfully engaged, our minds bring laser beam-like attention to the matter at hand. Head follows heart. Hence, the axiom:

Where the heart goes, the rest is sure to follow.

Where the heart grazes, the mind gazes. Where our heart finds sustenance—feeding and nurturing itself—our mind follows suit: fantasizing, day-dreaming, imagining and planning the fulfillment of the heart's appeals. When the heart is somewhere else, the mind spins thoughts, ponder-ings, musings about the object of our heart's attention. Head follows heart.

121

If you're doing something that isn't where your head is then feel into your heart. Shift your *mind*-focus to *heart*-focus. You won't be able to fully concentrate on anything until your heart gets the attention it deserves.

If you've done something "wrong-headed" or "absent-minded," re-orient yourself to be "right-hearted."

Rather than getting your "head in the game," get your heart in on the action. When a coach riles up his players at half-time because his team is down by 10 and playing distractedly—as if the players' heads are elsewhere—what's his remedy? A motivational speech to inspire, to impassion, to connect with their *hearts*!

The coach doesn't break down the logic of the situation. He doesn't preach the facts and figures, run the play-by-play. He doesn't quote stats to engage their minds. No. He digs deep, summoning a *heart-felt* sermon to fire them up from *within*. He wins their hearts so their minds and bodies follow. The team plays better in the second half because it is committed, it is inspired: the players' hearts are in the game.

When hearts are stirred, beings become present, focused and aware. Heart-engagement is what conjures magic and summons miracles. It's how our team plays their best to come from behind for the win. Head follows heart.

Where the heart goes, the rest is sure to follow.

While we readily follow our heads down errant paths, to follow our hearts is never an error. While the mind can whip us into a frenzy, dizzy us with distraction and flush us down a thought spiral, the heart cannot, will not, and shall never lead us astray.

You must follow your heart. Eventually. No matter what. It's inevitable. Inalienable. Essential. It's do-or-die. And here's why: When we don't follow our heart, it lets us know. Tasks don't get done, missions aren't accomplished, happiness and joy elude us.

Tuning into our hearts leads us, literally, to the heart of the matter. Rather than being bent on pursuing matters *outside* of us, we should strive to understand the essence *within* us. At our vital core.

And what *is* the matter? Your heart will tell you.

What is *essential*? Your heart surely knows.

How can you *focus*? Your heart can guide you.

The mind proffers thoughts of an imperative nature, tasks us with the necessary To-Do's, implores us to pay attention, impatient for us to do *something*. Even without a sound, our thoughts can be cacophonous.

By contrast, the heart is a subtle instrument: powerful, consistent, patient. Quietly and vigorously bidding us to follow its urgings. The head deludes itself, ignoring the heart at its own peril. It *thinks* it can overpower the heart. But nothing reigns over the heart. It is our most vital instrument. Without it, no *vitality*. Without it, no life.

To ignore a heart turns a person ugly: in thought, in word, in deed. Bitterness, anger, resentment build. Then that ugliness lashes out at those who heed the inclination of their hearts. For those who haven't, it's too much to face.

When we ignore the gentle insistence of our heart for too long, our body experiences the resultant consequences: our pump flutters and fails, its sustained beatings wane. When consequences grow grave, it ceases to beat.

Where the heart goes, the rest is sure to follow.

March to the beat of your own drummer—the heart—while you can. As our hearts sow so shall we reap. If we don't allow our hearts to sow, then there shall be nothing to feed them, nothing to keep them beating, nothing for them—or us—to reap. When our heart-urgings become dead to us, our hearts die along with them. And we cannot live without our hearts.

So take this moment, right now, as an opportunity to tune into the tender musings of your most beloved—and loving—instrument. If your head isn't in the game, if your thoughts are elsewhere, then take this chance to converse with your heart about the object of its attention — and affection.

Checking in with your heart is the *best* thing you can do today. It won't steer you wrong. It won't lead you astray. Chances are whatever is keeping you from your heart's desire is the *real* distraction. The bearings of our heart always lead us to truth.

So hear it, heed it, heart it so you can flip the script, transforming those common turns-of-phrase into uncommon awarenesses-of-heart.

How could I be so wrong-*headed*? —> I am right-hearted.

What was I *thinking*? —> What am I *feeling*?

I've got to get my *head* in the game! —> My *heart* is in for the win!

Where the heart goes, the rest is sure to follow.

You follow?

Truth Serum:
The heart conjures magic and summons miracles.
The bearing of our heart always leads us to Truth.

Fear Vs. Love

There are two primary energies in the Universe: Fear and Love.

We might think that it's Love and Hate, or Love and Anger, or Love and any other myriad emotion of the negative persuasion, but all negative aspects arise from the fundamental opposing force to Love — and that's Fear.

When one is in love, immersed in love, in tune with the vibration of love there is ease, happiness, empowerment, trust, effortlessness, joy, surrender, synchronicity, strength, courage, expansion. All manner of positive serendipities materialize.

When one is in the grip of fear, it is restrictive, reductive, diminishing, shrinking, narrowing, limiting and all manner of emotions that give rise to corollaries like hate, anger, jealousy, envy, bitterness, resentment, aggression, murder, war.

There is, however, a positive side to fear. Fear in itself isn't bad. Fear is an innate response that keeps us from danger, alerts us to imminent peril, sharpens our senses in its presence and stimulates our fight-or-flight response. It can keep us alive. It's a preponderance of fear—when that emotional vibration is sustained and fed—that causes damage.

Fear can be a great motivator. It's a trigger to get moving in the face of threat and the pressures of life. It pushes us to move from where we are to where we need to be. Fear can show us what we *don't* want so that we move in the direction of what we *do*.

In my experience, when fear arises in my dreams or visions, I take it as showing me possibilities that I *do not* want. Rather than obsess about them, I work in contrary fashion to what might cause those outcomes to arise.

For example, if my fear is that an important project I am relying on might fall through because I failed to meet a deadline or handle the details, rather than dwell on the finality of that outcome, I use fear as a motivator to get my butt in gear to complete the project in ample time so that the conditions for that fear to manifest are precluded. Should that outcome arise in any case, then at least I've done everything in my power to alter course and to fulfill my part of the equation.

Making decisions out of fear is never the best way to decide. Acting *in* fear, acting *from* fear, acting *fearfully* will never produce the optimal outcome nor your most desirable destiny. Never. Because deciding from a place of fear shows an absence of faith in a generously supportive Universe.

Choosing from fear is choosing from *perceived lack*, not from *infinite abundance*. Perception of lack says there just isn't enough — for you, for your neighbor, for everyone. And that's untrue. There is ample abundance for everyone's need, but not everyone's greed, as Gandhi proclaimed. And greed arises from fear: Fear of scarcity. That it's a zero sum game. That there are winners and losers and nothing in-between.

If you find yourself in fear, dig deeper. Try to excavate and discern what motivates your fright. Is it thinking you will never be loved? That you won't find a place to live as perfect as the place you're currently living? That you'll never find a job that pays as much as the one you're in? That the sense of community you have can never be replicated? That there is no way out of your present circumstances?

Probe into fear, examine it, embrace it, research it, don't shrink from it. Embrace it to understand why fear is present within you so that you can transform it to a higher vibration. When you find yourself drifting toward Fear, consciously put forth efforts to climb back toward Love.

Draw from Love's higher vibration *before* you make a move, make a decision or make a mistake because the vibration from which you decide will give rise to more of the same kind of vibe.

Truth Serum:

On Love
The heart is a thousand-stringed instrument
that can only be tuned with love.
~ Hafiz (a Sufi poet)

The vibration from which you decide
will give rise to the same kind of vibe.
~ Truth (yours truly)

On Fear
Fear is the cheapest room in the house.
I would like to see you living in better conditions.
~ Hafiz (still a Sufi poet)

Fear draws from limiting lack;
Love from infinite abundance.
~ Truth (still yours)

| ACTION |

Find your groove, but don't make it a rut.

~ Truth

Just Start

Growing up, if we stepped out of line, we've all seen a dad—our dad, a pal's dad, maybe or our dad's dad—who would warn us with a wag of their finger: "Don't start with me."

Well, here's some opposing counsel: JUST START.

No matter what you think you need, no matter what resources you wish you had, no matter what preparation you have yet to do... Just start, damnit. Just start.

The art of the start is self-defining: it's art when you start. If you don't start you'll have no art.

Gandhi advised that we "don't know what result will come from our actions, but if we don't act there will be no result." He also observed that when we set our minds to begin something, the universe makes ready the essential tools to accomplish that endeavor even if none were available when we started.

That's the science of art. It's a simple formula: Begin and the universe supports our efforts. But without the start, we're inert, static, unmoving. There's no catalyst for chemistry. Without the start, our only practice is procrastination. Hence to have art, *you must start*.

It's the start that gets the machinery turning. Putting ourselves in motion puts the universe in motion on our behalf. Creation wants to move, which is why it's *always* moving. And why stagnation feels so uncomfortable. If we're not learning, growing, expanding we are discomfited by our lack of progress. We go loco without locomotion. Which pushes us to move, to act, to do.

We must grow or decay, birth ourselves into existence or wither away. We can't stay the same or lie stagnant. Even sitting still is an illusion because the globe, the spheres, the cosmos is always moving — rotating, revolving, expanding, contracting, spinning, whirling, cyclonically, vortextually, perpetually.

We learn by doing. By getting grimy. By getting our clothes muddy. And our hands dirty. While we're at, let's redefine "getting our hands dirty," which shouldn't mean "stained with evidence" like the tragic Lady MacBeth wiping at the residue of her sanguinary act, "Out, out damned spot!" No. The crime is inertia. We *must* roll up our sleeves and thrust our digits into the earth. Soil our clothes. Get messy. And mess up.

If you want to change your life then you must change something ABOUT your life. To make alterations, you must alter *something*. If you desire transformation, you must transform your thoughts, your ways, yourself. The *thought* of change is the impetus. The *act* of making a change is motion.

If you are passive about change, you're life will *still* change. No matter what. But without your *active* participation, you won't have a say in the matter. You'll be swept along in the current.

You can fight *against* change, cling to stagnation, to the status quo. But get ready for discomfort because the rules are thus:

Pain results when you RESIST the change. Then change happens TO you while it changes the conditions of your life.

Empowerment results when you EMBRACE the change. Then change happens WITH you while it changes you.

Transformation results when you BECOME the change. Then the change IS you.

The fulcrum of change is the start. That's the art. Just start. Commence. Begin. There's transformational power available to you *right* now. There's movement in this very moment.

Want to start an exercise regime? Do ten push-ups *right now*. See how you feel. If you'd rather run, step out your door and sprint down the block. You don't need the right sweat suit, you don't need new running shoes and you don't need permission—or excuses.

More sleep? Go lie down. Take a nap. *Right now.*

Meditation sound cool, but you don't have any training? Put down your phone. Sleep your laptop. Place a bookmark in this page and lay it aside. Then sit up straight. Close your eyes. Breathe deeply for three breaths. Then three more. Then a final three. Focus solely on your breath. In and out. In and out. In and out. Open your eyes. Check in with how you feel. Better? Good. That's because 1) You meditated. 2) You just began a meditation practice. Now rinse and repeat.

Start start start.

Want to start representing athletes? Scout some talent. Want to open a gallery? Hang some art. Want to start throwing pottery? Turn the wheel. Want to eat healthier? Crunch a carrot. Want to start a blog? Write something and publish it. Want to build something? Grab some Legos.

Just do it. Do it now. It's not "fake it till you make it," it's "FATE IT till you make it."

Start what you desire to do and you'll find out PDQ (pretty darn quick) if you like it, if you're any good at it, what it takes to do it well (to do it at all), and whether it's a vocation, an avocation, a fantasy unfulfilled or a fulfilling fantasy.

Take baby steps and the Universe responds with applause. Like a toddler learning to walk who ventures a couple of uneven, wobbly steps, you may land your tush, but you get adulation and smiles from supporters, a pick-me-up and encouragement to try again. Wouldn't it be great if everything we attempted was like learning to walk?

Imagine if a baby waited until it had the balance, coordination, muscular development and instruction to make the attempt. If it waited for the perfect conditions. For privacy so as not to risk embarrassment.

Ridiculous.

Same goes for you. What are you waiting for? Waiting for all there is to know? Until the timing is "perfect?" Waiting for the world to be ready? That's all bullshit. It will never be "ready" and you can never be ready enough. Prepared, yes, but we must learn as we go because that's how it works: no matter how prepared we are, life confronts us with the unexpected, the unanticipated, the unusual. Unsurprisingly.

We *must* learn by doing. By launching. By attempting. Through trial-and-error. Through trial-and-failure. Through trial-by-fire. That's how we hone our skills, fire our earthenware, bake our cookies. We make. We measure. We learn. Then we iterate and make-measure-learn again. It never ends. There is no other way.

Waiting is inaction. It's the *opposite* of starting: it's stopping. So get the ball rolling. Don't gather the moss of immobility. The only one who can give you the green light you're waiting on is *you*. So, Gentlepersons, start your engines.

And remember, despite Dad's contrary advice, even Papa was a rollin' stone.

Truth Serum:
Fate it till you make it.

You Can't Go Wrong

What a nice thought. If only it were true...

But it is. You can't go wrong. No matter what.

When options present themselves and you have to choose between something good or something better and you find yourself indecisive? Realize you can't go wrong.

In life, you just can't go wrong. Or make a mistake. All you have are options. "Good" choices are rewarded with good experiences. A reinforcement of what led you to make them. Of the practice of discernment. Of sound decision-making. Bravo. "Bad" choices—or "mistakes"—create an opportunity to grow. To refine. To practice perspicacity.

It's like choosing the "right" color for your new car. Hey, it's a *new* car. You can't go wrong.

It's like deciding to find out when pregnant if you're having a boy or girl. Hey, your having a child. You can't go wrong.

It's like picking between your favorite flavors of ice cream. Mint chip won't take offense if you go with the caramel swirl. You can't go wrong.

Just like life. Even though we feel we've gone wrong, made a mistake or taken a misstep, we haven't. We're living life the way it was intended: by being human.

The nature of human existence is a risk. That you ventured here as a soul from Source energy is emblematic of your willingness to take the trip, to buy the ticket for this Earth-bound roller coaster ride.

Makes you gulp when you climb aboard. Butterflies flit in your stomach as the safety harness pins your shoulders to the seat, gripping you tight for the chills and spills to come. Your heart pounds in your chest. This decision feels... risky, frisky, frightening. But, oh, do you feel so alive!

As the coaster ascends into the sky you're filled with dread or exuberance. Anticipation gets the pulse going. Maybe you're gonna like it. Maybe you're not. Maybe you're gonna puke. Maybe not. Maybe you'll scream. And enjoy screaming. Or maybe not. Whatever happens, happens. But you're committed — at least for the length of the drop and some G-force-inducing whirls.

Nevertheless, you can't go wrong. It's a no-lose proposition. A new life experience. You'll know what riding this particular roller coaster feels like. And you'll either want to do it again, you'll want to try another one — higher, with more loop-de-loops — or maybe you'll find a ride that's more your speed. Whatever the outcome, you'll learn, you'll grow, you'll have a brush with drama and some fun with fright. You'll make it out alive. And live to ride another day.

Moving on. You can't go wrong.

There are no mistakes. Only decisions and outcomes and then better ones. Or worse ones. Doesn't matter. It all works out in the end. Nothing is forever. The nature of reality is impermanence. Just like the roller coasters of life are fleeting, so is life itself.

If you don't like the ride you're on, pick another one. Choose a different amusement. Change your life. Start anew.

And if you *do* love it, then don't leave it. Rinse and repeat. Ride those rails. Enjoy that coaster again and again. Laugh till you drop. Scream your head off. Close the park.

Whatever you choose, you can't go wrong.

What a relief.

Truth Serum:
If life's roller coaster makes you sick, opt for a new amusement. Whichever ride you choose, you can't go wrong.

Courage

Courage is action in the face of uncertain outcome.

Courage flies in the face of fear. It's not the *absence* of fear, but the acknowledgement that fear is a reductive vibration. One that is retreating, reducing, shrinking. If one wishes to expand, one must embrace a different vibration — courage.

Courage stems from love. Love begets trust. Trust that the Universe's divine love will support you and guide and protect you and nurture you and deliver you to something more and better. Something that will serve your highest aspiration for yourself and enable you to become the greatest version of you.

That an outcome is uncertain is just how things are. It's the state of things. Nothing is certain, even when we think it must be. In the same way the cosmos may hold an outcome we can't possibly predict, it holds opportunity for us we couldn't possibly see or create for ourselves unless we step into its grace with loving trust. We must embrace uncertainty, welcome the unknown.

For what is courage than running headlong into certain death? Venturing toward certain failure? Embracing certain demise?

The Universe is all powerful and it has an ironic sense of humor. The best laid plans of mice and men come undone in the mighty hand of All That Is. God likes to turn expectation on its ear, such is the nature of His creativity. So He delivers us from "certain" death. Rescues us from failure. Spares us demise.

And how did things turn out that way? Who could have predicted it? No one. And that's the point. Even though the outcome is "certain," don't count the Universe out. Don't dare God. Because He's up to the challenge. And so are you.

Because of this, we are encouraged to choose courage over fear in every single instance without fail. Because God wants us to be bold. "The Universe rewards you for taking risks on its behalf." "Fortune favors the brave." So why choose fear? Growth does not arise from fear. Wealth does not arise from fear. Life does not arise from fear.

A good litmus test is to evaluate the alternative in the face of fear: if you're feeling fear, if something you desire requires courage, then it's likely that current conditions must remain status quo to remain in fear. In other words, even though present conditions might be painful, they are known to us and there is comfort in what is "known." Therefore, this is our "comfort zone of discomfort."

But dissatisfaction, disillusionment, dismay are elements that motivate us to make a shift into the unknown or out of our comfort zone of discomfort in order to change our present circumstances. Fear of the unknown keeps us from it. Fear of the unknown keep us in discomfort. Fear keeps us in a state of suffering.

Courage is the urge to catapult us from all that. The notion of possibility. The "What if?" What if there is something better in store for me? What if I can find my true calling doing something else somewhere else? What if I can find a loving partner more in sync with me? What if there's more to the world than this little slice of it? More to life than everything up to this moment that I've been brought up to believe?

Guess what? The answer to all those questions is "Yes!" Life is boundless. It holds infinite potentiality. "To have hope is to have everything."

Hope is the catalyst of courage. To hope is to entertain the possibilities. It's what can light the fire to get you out there and to get things moving in another direction, to find a better way, another light, a different path.

To have courage is the willingness to try to uncover them. To trust. To venture in the direction of possibility. By doing so, you take a small step towards the Divine. Then the Divine takes a giant leap towards you.

The truth is that *all* outcomes are uncertain. Even those we predict with 99.9% accuracy sometimes surprise us in their ability to go "pear-shaped" (as the Brits are fond of saying). And a pear may not be the low-hanging fruit you sought to pluck.

Courage is venturing into uncharted realms. Like Christopher Columbus or Amerigo Vespucci (after whom America is named), courage lays in wait to be discovered on the *other* side of fear, which may appear as vast as an ocean.

You've heard the adage "the only way out is through." Well, here it is in effect. To get *to* courage you have to make your way *through* fear. Move *through* fear into greater realms where the Divine shines its light on those who embrace uncertainty through the courage of belief, the mettle of character, the resolve of trust.

Maybe there's a continent out there with *your* name on it.

Truth Serum:
To get to *courage you have to make your way* through *fear.*

Don't Diss Courage

What does it take to accomplish something new, something different, something innovative, fresh, creative? To manifest and fabricate a dream from scratch? To birth it into existence and put it out there for others to react to? It takes *courage*.

When someone is in the process of creating, that's what they are harnessing, building up and powering themselves with — courage. So when an artist or creator or entrepreneur or inventor or child shares their idea with you in a nascent stage, when you *discourage* them, you are debilitating them by taking away the very element they need to create — their courage. You are *dissing* courage. Dissing *someone else's* courage to be precise. You're not criticizing. You're not being constructive. You're not sharing your opinion. You are dissing someone else's own courageous act of faith.

The counter to this is to *encourage*. When you encourage, you aren't just rooting someone on, you are bolstering their courage. You are empowering them through the force of mettle, bravery and endeavor to push through, to continue on their path of creativity, to push forward to find success. Rather than thwart the process of creativity in the Universe, you are contributing to it and promoting it in a very specific way — through the energy of courage itself.

Can you imagine discouraging a seedling as it tried to set down its root in the earth? As it attempted to sprout through the soil in a courageous act of life? Who is another to pass judgment on the sprout's potential? On the seedling's capability to rise to the full glory of an epic redwood that could live thousands of years? Imagine if the seedling was *discouraged* as it started out, belittled as it had just begun to grow.

To create is our native instinct. It's our ground state of being. We unlearn how to do it naturally and effortlessly and prolifically because we learn judgment and criticism and humility. So it takes courage to return to ourselves and to our natural abilities. When we do what comes naturally, it is a courageous act.

To diss courage is an act of cowardice. *Dis*couragement is anti-courageous and demonstrates one's own lack of bravado. To encourage another being is to act on and to display one's own courage. Courage begets courage. Cowardice begets discouragement. As you sow so shall you reap.

Encouraging courage is a courageous act. So be courageous! Be bold! In the same way the best way to cheer yourself up is by cheering up someone else, the best way to bolster your own courage is to encourage someone else.

Anything that enhances courage, enhances life. Because courage is taking steps in the face of an uncertain outcome. And it's all uncertain. Even if we think something is certain, nothing is. Anything can happen and usually does. Courage overcomes the resistance of fear and prevents it from stopping the flow of creativity, from halting evolution.

An act of courage is an act of love. An act of *dis*courage-ment is an act of fear. Fear is the opposite of love. If you are discouraging another then you are doing so from a place of your own fear. And you are allowing your fear to control your actions, to spread itself like an infection.

Treat discouragement like the infirmity that it is, the debilitation it attempts to be. Prevent its spread to others by being courageous. Praise, embolden, raise up or inspire another. One simple act is enough to dismiss the fear within yourself because it enables you to see what's possible for another. Envisioning possibilities enhances your view of the world to allow for the infinite love of the Universe to reach you, to reach them, and to work its magic.

Even though the Tin Man was looking for a heart, it was the Lion's desire for courage that led to love. Because the path to courage *is* the path to love. As Gandhi professed, love is a courageous act: "A coward is incapable of exhibiting love; it is the prerogative of the brave."

Love is our prerogative. Our privilege. Our birthright. We are born to love. We are made to love. As Rumi ventured: "We have not come into this exquisite world to hold ourselves hostage from love... But to experience ever and ever more deeply our divine courage, freedom and light!"

Love is the prerogative of the brave, courage is the hallmark of the Divine. To diss courage is to deny another's—and one's own—divinity. To deny our divinity is to refuse the loving role we were conceived to play as if "to the manner born."

To discourage is human; to encourage, Divine.

Truth Serum:
Love is the prerogative of the brave;
courage the hallmark of the Divine.
*   *   *

The path to courage is the path to love.

Act Without Despair

Joan Baez said, "Action is the antidote to despair." True. Don't just sit there and despair. Act. But act *without* despair. Because action coupled with despair is *desperation*.

It's important to act. But it's more important to act with trust. With faith. With a sense of confidence that the Universe will support you. With a sense of humor, a sense of belief, a sense of fun that no matter how things work out, they'll work out for the best. Know that events and outcomes assist you on your journey of learning. And give you something to laugh at, even if it's yourself

So take action. Act swiftly. Act even if you're faking it—or "fating it"—till you make it. Act with gratitude for all the help you receive along the way from individuals, from creation, from forces seen and unseen, perceived and hidden, that coalesce their energies to assist you in eventually overcoming your present challenge.

Don't take action with a reductive, retreating, recoiling lack of confidence because it attracts what you DO NOT want. When we act with a sense of despair or dread or fear it gives off an odious scent—a vibratory quality—that others can sense. When we appear desperate, when we feel desperate, we make poor decisions. Our despair misguides our actions, propelling them in errant directions resulting in *acts of desperation*.

Desperation is a consequence of feeling the inevitability of our demise rather than the certitude of our ascension. Ascension is improvement, a rising up, a betterment of our circumstances. And if not "ascension" perhaps "accession" applies. Accession means the attainment of a position (like the Presidency or a promotion or partnership), or acceptance to a group (like the PTA or Alumni Association or athletic team or book club), which is often what we're desperately seeking.

Desperation, on the other hand, is a last ditch effort. Helpless and clamoring. It's a dying breath. A final whimper. A panicked, clutching, grasping attempt made in vain.

Desperation is easy to sense because it smells like fear. And it is. Like fear, it often does the *opposite* of what you desire. It doesn't attract salvation, rescue, positivity or opportunity. It repels them. It drives away the people, projects and partnerships that *will* help you. What it attracts are more conditions that created your despair in the first place.

When rational, caring people (the only people from whom you want help in desperate circumstances) tune into your being, they'll sense desperation. What's the first thing a rational, caring person does in the face of your feeling desperate? They calm you down. Get you to breathe, to center, to settle. To acknowledge that everything will be fine. That help is on the way. That the problem can and will be resolved. *Then* they offer help. Rationally. Carefully.

The danger of desperation is that those who prey on circumstance, those who don't have your best interests at heart, can also sense your desperation. Desperation signals that you are a ripe target. They may swoop in under the guise of helping you to take advantage of you. And that's the opposite of what you need. It makes your situation worse and more desperate!

So don't despair. ACT. But don't act in despair. Because that's DESPERATION. Not only is not effective, but it's not attractive, as any blind date will tell you.

If you're in desperation you're expending a lot of perspiration, risking manipulation and intimidation while hoping for consideration.

So remedy desperation with a big inhale and exhalation. Some meditation. (Not medication!) Contemplation. Cogitation. Then, with a confident foundation, act from a higher vibration. And that will yield your best manifestation.

Good cause for celebration.

Get my intimation?

Truth Serum:
Desperation is a consequence of feeling the inevitability of our demise rather than the certitude of our ascension.

Action Expresses Priorities

In architecture there's a concept called a Truth Window. It is an opening in the interior wall of a building that reveals the materials with which the wall is made. This is particularly interesting if, for example, the walls are constructed of straw bales, an uncommon material with only a few artisans capable of building with it.

For a homeowner who boasts to guests about this unorthodox method and straw bales' efficacy for drainage and insulation, the disbeliever and inquisitor alike can glimpse the homeowner's claims through a "Truth Window."

What are your own windows to Truth? Can you identify them in yourself? Can you identify them in others?

Our Truth Window provides a glimpse into the heart of our own Truth regardless of our words or our behavior. Gandhi has a simple axiom that cuts to the heart of the matter, one which is the highest and clearest expression of our intention: "Action expresses priorities."

Regardless of what we say or what we mean in the moment we say it, our best intention, our promises, our bargaining, our negotiation, our excuses, our explanations... our *actions* are our clearest window to Truth.

Often in business, I'll hear from clients dismayed that an executive claimed to like their project in the room, but failed to make an offer on it. "But they said... they *loved* it. They were going to buy it!" To which Gandhi's tenet perfectly applies: Action Expresses Priorities. If the executive was truly interested, she would buy the project. It doesn't matter what was she conveyed in the moment or if she even meant it at the time. What do the executive's actions (or inaction) express? *The project is not her priority.*

145

How often have we heard ourselves say, "This is important to me. This is a priority. It's at the top of my list." And we may even believe it when we say it. But then something else comes up, other concerns take precedence and the person or project or task to which we had committed gets pushed down our list or falls off it entirely.

Action Expresses Priorities.

If it were important enough, it'd get done. No matter how we wish it when we say it, if it isn't a priority, it doesn't get our attention.

So our *actions* are a Truth Window. In contrast to our words or our intention, actions are the real cut-through. The undeniable, inalienable, absolute truth.

This axiom applies to our personal relationships. When someone is a priority, you get there, you get it done, you make it happen. If there's romantic potential and it's someone you *really* want to connect with, you'll make it your number one priority, rearrange your day, shift a meeting, postpone an appointment, cancel on a friend... to magically and "coincidentally" run into your romantic interest wherever they may be. You show up. You're there. Inevitably, you appear.

Action Expresses Priorities.

You want to be there—because it's *that* important—so you are. Same holds true for a family member in distress. If they are vital enough to you, you'll show up for them. You'll cross the country. You'll incur great expense. You'll make it your business to be there.

Or if your child is in need. Or injures themselves. Or has a school project that has to get done on time because it's a third of their grade in the class. Guess what? You're up all night to care for them or to help them hot glue that class assignment.

Action Expresses Priorities.

What about follow-through? What about completing projects? What about getting shit done? There are always a million excuses why something couldn't be done, can't be done, hasn't been done. And yet, if it's important enough, urgent enough, priority enough, it happens.

In fact, the potential *excuse* for incompletion is actually the potential *boast* for how awesome you are and what great follow-through you have for delivering.

Imagine you have a two-day turnaround to rewrite a presentation and to deliver an incredible pitch for an important meeting and during that time you're under the weather, your dog has to go the vet, your mother in-law arrives for a visit and you get a flat tire... All wonderful excuses for not getting it done. Totally understandable, right? Or... you could accomplish the task in spite of all those distractions, and thus, your achievement becomes a bragging right of sorts, even if you keep the brag to yourself. All that crap going on and you were still able to follow-through! You completed the goal. Your personal point of pride can be enjoyed in the wake of success. Phew.

The alternative is to *not* be prepared, to *not* have succeeded, to have waded through all those distractions and *still* have to complete the project, but behind schedule. You've let yourself down, you've let others down, you're in a shame spiral of justification for why you couldn't follow through. The real reason it didn't get done: because it wasn't priority enough.

Action Expresses Priorities.

Instead, turn the excuse into a bragging right. "Despite the detractors, I still made it happen! Despite the distractions — success!" Why? Because it was important for me to do so.

Action Expresses Priorities.

Ever miss a plane flight for a vacation because you couldn't pack your bag in time or you were too tired to wake up for it? Doubtful.

Somehow, that vacation is a priority. Especially if you nailed that presentation. Even if you're packing late into the night (like I always am) and set the alarm for three hours after you've finally gone to sleep (like I always do), you're getting up in time to make your flight.

Action Expresses Priorities.

Our clearest Truth Window, the one without any reflective glare or fog on the glass, is action. Our actions tell the Truth, reveal the Truth, confirm the Truth.

Action Expresses Priorities.

Ain't that the Truth.

Truth Serum:
When action expresses priorities, your excuse for not getting it done becomes your boast for making it happen.

Make Peace With the Outcome

In any negotiation, in any life event, in any situation where there is anticipation, there is expectation. Our expectations are met, exceeded or reality falls short. If we prime ourselves for these three possible outcomes and "make peace" with each, we are prepped for happiness and girded for *any* outcome by a sense of equanimity and acceptance.

Making peace with the outcome means that we are prepared for the worst, but expecting the best. We are cautiously optimistic, as opposed to enthusiastically pessimistic. And since we are fine with all eventualities — whatever happens, happens — we can enter our negotiation, go on our date, launch our venture, make our investment, embark on our activity, commitment, interview, audition or performance with a different mindset. "This *will* work out," we assure ourselves, "No matter what." Because we are personally serene with the result — whatever the result may be.

"Making peace" means *peace-making*: creating, cultivating and perpetuating calm, composure, concord. Which starts and ends with you. Peace presupposes you are not at war with yourself. Because where outcomes are concerned *you* are the only person with whom you can be at war. So give yourself a break. Allow *what is* to be *what is;* allow *what is to be* to be.

When the Buddha speaks of detachment, he means one is at ease in *all* circumstances; one has made peace with any and all scenarios, probabilities, likelihoods. One accepts how things are and allows what emerges to emerge.

It may take some wrestling with yourself to get there. You may have to tangle with entanglements. Grapple with grapplers. Head-butt heads. Throw down before throwing in the towel. Ultimately, though, the battle is *within*, not without.

And not without merit: it's a peace *process*. We must go through the ups and downs to make peace with the result. Being Buddha-like is no walk in the park. Unless you *are* Buddha, in which case life is precisely a walk in the park. An eternal, peaceful frolic through the tulips. It can be for us, as well, but one must be completely at ease, in unperturbed acceptance of what is, not struggling against what is not.

As Gandhi professed, "There is no path to peace. Peace is the path." One can best *make* peace by being *at* peace. How can there be peace in the world if we are in a psychological state of pique? How can we settle the waters of conflict if our inner pool of resources is turbulent?

Peace isn't settled from protracted negotiations. It's not based on contingency nor compromise. There's no external causation that adds up to internal equanimity. Peace is a state of pure being. A process that starts *within* us. Which is why prepping ourselves for peace is a practice, a discipline, an attitude that empowers us to greet anything that comes our way with aplomb.

Whether we do this in *anticipation* of a negotiation, while *in the midst* of an entanglement, or when we're in the *aftermath* of an outcome is unimportant. When we've made peace with *all* outcomes we disallow *any* income to cause us disquiet. And making peace leaves room for all potentialities. It doesn't limit the result. It doesn't dampen the upside.

Making peace still leaves room for "happily surprised."

Truth Serum:
Making peace with the outcome
means making peace with the income
* * *

Where outcomes are concerned you are
the only one with whom you can be at war.

150

Decency

We have a choice in how we handle our affairs, especially the tough stuff: firings, break-ups, cast-offs. We choose to handle something to the best of our ability — or the worst. As one of my favorite Cornell professors advised, "If you have to fire someone, make sure it's the best thing you do that day."

The *best* thing. Handled in the best way possible. Not as an afterthought. Not when you're tired. Not after a bad night's sleep. Not squeezed in just before the close of the business. The best thing. No exceptions.

Not saying it's easy. Or that it's fun. But we know when we're giving something our all. And why should we give the tough stuff any less than our best? Then we're doing our-selves—and the other party—a disservice.

The measure of this effort can be thought of as *decency*. What constitutes "decent?" It's not exceptional. It's not stratospheric. It's not fantastic or amazing. But it's fair. It's correct. It's reasonable. A decent sandwich. A decent movie. A decent deal. A decent human being.

Decent is equitable. Just. Honorable. Respectable. Doable. Achievable. An attainable aspiration. A minimum re-quirement. Decent is not a high bar. It's within arm's reach. We don't even need to stretch for it.

Everyone has their own barometer, but our own take on "decent" should be something we'd put to the Pepsi Chal-lenge against another's sense of the word.

On a daily basis, do we treat our teammates, our co-workers, our siblings, our employees, our neighbors, our classmates, our family, ourselves, the public... with *decency*? Honorably? With a measured sense of what's right and just?

The intention we carry is the party favor we end up carry-ing away. By simply treating others the way we would like to be treated, we set the stage for the outcome we expect. If we *expect* a fight, for example, we're likely to get one. If we enter the fray with fists up and the other party enters unawares, someone is leaving with a black eye. And it might not be the someone we expected.

As a litmus test to measure how corrosively we carry out our duties, let's ask ourselves if we've done the "decent" thing. Once we've let someone go, left someone behind, left the dance with someone other than who brought us, do we reflect on our treatment of that fellow traveler as *decent*? If the answer is "no," then there is room for doing better. For doing right. For being more human. Thus, more *humane*.

A metric for whether we behaved "decently" is to flip the script. As when we negotiate, if it's such a "good deal" then we should be happy to take whatever we're selling on the terms we're offering. Buying someone out of a partnership, a project, a business, a marriage? If it's a decent deal then it's a deal we must be willing to accept ourselves.

The converse is also true: with decent deal-making we should be happy to offer what we're asking. It's not a take-as-much-as-you-can-get game, but an equitable-for-all-concerned approach. If we wouldn't want the deal we're insisting upon, then maybe it ain't so decent after all.

Letting someone go? Based on our handling of the matter, would *we* feel crushed or encouraged leaving the office for the last time? Picture it: Parking lot. Loading the car with a boxful of photos from our desk. Our favorite stapler. Are we flipping-off the building on our way out or offering gratitude for this latest chapter?

Choosing one firm over another? One superstar candidate over other contenders? How would we feel after finding out we're *not* the firm chosen or the individual hired? Do we allow hope to brew or resentments to stew?

Another barometer is to ask oneself how we'd feel in the other person's shoes. Pretty easy. Just pretend you're the one it's all happening to. You're last to be picked. You're left on the bench. You're getting dumped. You're passed over for the promotion. You're cast off in favor of the *next* best thing.

How would you want to be told? How would you want to be treated? The news isn't pretty. It sucks, actually. But do you want the intel delivered in the typical way: To find out through others, to overhear it, to read it in a Tweet? Or would you want it straight on the chin? To have a real conversation, to be told fairly and honorably? Chances are the way you delve it out will be the way it comes back to you down the road. As we sow...

But it's ingrained in us to act from *fear*. Fear that the other person will take it poorly. So we come up with excuses for our lack of tact: They'll sue us. Criticize us. Badmouth us. Or take the opportunity to do us harm. They'll yell and scream and sabotage the company, the enterprise, the whole shebang if we choose to handle a bad situation with aplomb. Or maybe there's not enough time to handle it with tact, or maybe they're not worth the effort, or we're firing them anyway, or booting them from the team... why should it be the *best* thing we do today? Shouldn't it be the *opposite*?

We've all witnessed circumstances where the end result would be *exactly* the same except if it had been handled decently there would be no hard feelings.

We've all been on the receiving end of a harsh outcome fostering bitter sentiments. Instead of well-wishes and amicable partings, a string of privately-spoken expletives follows an earnest wish that those responsible die horrible deaths. The sooner the better.

Comeuppance is *not* something to have wished upon you. Instead, reach for an outcome where the spurned party has gratitude for the manner in which things were handled.

They may not be happy with the result, but a compassionate course of action is something for which everyone can be grateful. The conclusion will be the same: they are dumped, jilted, fired, divorced, jettisoned, excommunicated, expelled or expunged. But instead of wishing you dead, they'll wish there were more decent people like you.

Decency makes a difference. The opposite of decent is *in*decent, which is a *descent*. A downward slope. The low road. Which is long, dark and dreary. While the view from the high road is... decent.

Whether high or low, our road through difficult situations, tough choices and uncomfortable decisions can be lined with flower petals or broken glass. Decency sets our *soles* on the gentler path. Decency is gentler on the *soul*.

Truth Serum:
Decency lines the path with flower petals rather than broken glass. And what's good for the sole is good for the soul.

Who Do You Work For?

Okay. Here's a Cosmic Law: if you work on behalf of the Universe, it will work on behalf of you. If you advocate for the Universe, it will advocate for you.

This means exercising your creativity and your trust. The Universe is divinely creative. It *wants* to stretch your capacity to trust in the magnitude of its magnanimous nature. This kind of trust in the cosmos and an active, continual practice of good works on behalf of the Divine (essentially, exercising one's *own* divinity) is fundamental to spirituality, Faith, and, by extension, religion.

Which is to say, if you work on behalf of God, God will work on behalf of you. If you work on behalf of Christ, or Christ Consciousness, Christ will work on your behalf. If you do the work of the Buddha by demonstrating your Buddha-like nature, then the unseen forces that feed and support those Buddha-like energies will support you.

When you act in the way of Zen, then the equanimous forces of Zen work on your behalf. When you embody the teachings of Muhammad, then Allah will lay blessings along your path. When one allows Great Spirit to work through oneself, miracles happen and we are sustained and nurtured and held to the bosom of Great Spirit. When we act on behalf of Loving Consciousness we benefit from the largesse of Loving Consciousness.

Call it what you will, but acting on behalf of, with the intention of and in the interest of the Divine fills our coffers with Divine blessings, gifts, bestowings and spoils. It's a rule. An axiom. A universal truth. What goes around comes around. As one sows, so shall one reap. The love you make is equal to the love you take.

Sounds simplistic. And it is. Reciprocity. God *does* pay it back. In this life or the next. The good works you sow here and now will reap rewards—the real kind, the spiritual kind, the substantive, substantial, sustaining kind—in this life or the next. Believe it.

All we need to do is pay it out, pay it forward, pay it mind. We shouldn't covet, hog or squander our riches. We shouldn't let parsimony rule the day, trickling out our blessings in the smallest of tight-fisted quantities. And we mustn't linger on lack or lack returns to us, lack expands for us; we receive *less*.

Therefore, get more of what you're working toward with each deposit into the spiritual bank. Throw generosity and gratitude, kindness and beneficence into your account and you can draw on it with interest. Deposit avarice and stinginess, cruelty and covetousness and you'll have oodles of the same to draw from — and drown in.

Like the most generous corporation we could work for, our good works result in Divine dividends, stock options and generous annuities—gifts, blessings, rewards and benefactions that keep on giving—as long as we continue to bestow our own gifts on others, on Creation, on behalf of the Creator.

We can't ask when it will come back. Or how much will return to us. Or what kind of reciprocity we'll be receiving because it's *energetic*. The Universe is a universal gift-giver: infinitely abundant and creative in the types of presents it bestows upon us and how. We receive its gifts in myriad forms. In forms we wouldn't expect. In forms we could never anticipate.

Perhaps you'll receive perfect health and longevity in return for your work. The real wealth is health, after all. Plenty of others would trade their entire fortunes for good health. If you have it, perhaps you've earned it or perhaps you can continue to earn it by working on behalf of All That Is.

In any given situation ask yourself, "What would God do?" Intuit how God might. And then act on God's behalf. When you do, you're guaranteed a divine flood of miraculous support for your efforts.

So take it on faith and trust that you'll be taken care of fairly, that things will be accounted for and held in balance, that you will be generously compensated for your efforts on behalf of the Creator.

The beautiful irony of working for this CEO is that He's constantly, continually, beneficently working on behalf of *you*.

Truth Serum:
If you work on behalf of the Universe,
it will work on behalf of you.

Unseen = Unmet = Unloved

We all just want to be loved. Fundamentally. That's it. For what is love other than feeling seen by others and being met where we're standing, dancing, playing, cooking, writing, singing, running, kicking, swimming, climbing, flying?

To feel unloved is to feel unseen. To be unmet. Unmet where we are. And invisible. If we were greeted with a big hug each morning when we walked into the office, we'd feel better about our day from the get-go. We'd be met. We'd feel seen. Alas, hugs aren't allowed in the workplace.

When we are feeling unseen, it's like people aren't getting it. Aren't getting us. We think: what's wrong with this picture? What's so hard to get? Why am I not being witnessed? What did I do wrong? What can I change about *me*?

Funny that our first inclination is that it's all about us and that we should alter something about ourselves in order to be loved. But that's an erroneous proposition. It stems from feeling unseen for who we *are*, who we *think* we are, who we *want* to be. So we feel the need to change ourselves in order to be seen, heard, accepted.

A friend once called me "The Invisible Man" when I was feeling most invisible to the world, in my community and in my working environment. Her words echoed a phrase I had been muttering to myself: *I'm invisible.*

She said it without ill-intent, but it crystallized what I was feeling. I had been using my best words, my most precise language, to explain who I was and why to people who couldn't receive my message or comprehend my communiqué. It felt as if I was blowing a dog whistle, but no one in sight could hear it.

The Invisible Man.

Being called "invisible" meant I was finally being seen. Seen, paradoxically, as *unseen*. This comment woke me up. I had to do something about it. So I endeavored to find a community of like-minds who *could* see me, who *would* see me, who *did* see me without my having to say anything. Tacitly. Wordlessly. Seen for who I was. Seen for who I am. Seen for who I was to become.

This community intuitively knew me better than the people at whom I was blowing my dog whistle. It was a tremendous feeling of connection. A deep accord. Love, at last, and sweet relief: From unseen to seen.

Which brings us to the *meeting* part. Being "unmet" means we're going the distance and no one is meeting us half-way, part-way, or enough of the way to be meaningful. To make us feel meaningful. To feel met. Feeling unmet means that we've crossed the gap, but no one is waiting for us on the other side. We're trekked the dark tunnel, but no one is standing in the light. Except us. Alone.

We must be met where we are right now. Not where we'll be in five to ten years (or days or minutes), but met exactly where we are at THIS VERY MOMENT. And that comes down to attention. Being present. In the here and now. For us and for those whom we hope to meet.

Who in our life is willing to meet us where we are right now? However we're feeling. However we're behaving. However low or high or silly or serious or distressed and worried or positive and cocky we are. Because that's what being met is. If someone can't match our mood or at least accept us in our present state of being, there's dissonance. If we're up, it brings us down; if we're down, we drop lower.

Which is why it's a two-way street to the meet-up. We can't expect everyone to come to us, we've got to journey to them, too, otherwise *they* are in a state of being unmet. And we know how that feels.

So we meet others half-way, along the path, down the alley, through the gateway, mid-tunnel, across town, across country, across the boardroom, the classroom or even the dining room. Whatever the bridge to the meet-up may be, to make a meeting work we've got to do our part and the other party has to do theirs. We take the journey to meet another and in so doing we are met.

In this way, we build a bridge to love. By doing our best to see others we honor who they truly are, deeply, at their core. And then we take strides to meet that person where they stand. With the hope that each step we take toward them, they'll take a step toward us.

Love, then, is found at the center of this bridge of being met, paved by the magic of being seen. We see, we meet, we love and in turn we are seen, we are met, we are loved.

That's the path to the "Beloved" as Sufi poets, Hafiz and Rumi, referred to God, the Creator, the Divine.

Be Seen => Be Met => Be Loved.

That's how we Be Long.

Truth Serum:
Love is found on the bridge of being met,
paved by the magic of being seen.

CHILD'S PLAY

To be a life-long student… is prudent.

~ Truth

Treat Everyone Like Children

Even though this may sound like a degrading way to treat another, it's actually the opposite. And a perfect way of being in the world.

Treat everyone like a child. Which is to say, with the utmost kindness, consideration and humanity. With patience and a sense of humor. With play and heart and hugs.

You will likely have to repeat yourself. Often. A good joke or a worthwhile lesson or a captivating story is worth repeating, after all. Be in the moment. Choose laughter as your ground state. Cry if it hurts. Wipe away tears quickly and easily. Sing-song thoughts or lessons or important matters to recall the teaching and to make them stick in your memory.

And why not? After all, we're *all* God's children. We are all babes born to the Universe. Sheer zygotes on a cosmic time-scale.

When passing a tottering toddler or babe in a stroller or tucked-in tot in its parent's arms, is our first thought to take advantage of that little being? Or is to recognize the big, soulful spirit in a pint-sized package? Do we plan to elicit a smile or tears? Connect or disengage? Spew acid or spout sweetness? Sprinkle salt or sugar?

Same thing with "grown-ups." As each one passes think of them as little children making their way in the world. Each encounter is a unique experience that could shape their way of being. Each moment is fresh, born anew.

Don't intimidate, lessen, criticize, burden, frighten or scold. Instead, enlighten, enliven and empower. Elicit a smile. Create a connection. Offer an olive branch. Make a new friend.

Treat everyone like children and maybe they'll do the same for you. And one day we'll all celebrate a birthday in the park where we're all young at heart.

Truth Serum:
Treat everyone like children and maybe they'll do the same for you. After all, we're all God's children.

Make. Believe.

What is make-believe? It's a term applied to children. To their play. The power within that simple directive is everything we need to know to power our dreams into creation. We make what we believe.

When we "make-believe" we create our reality by fantasizing parameters, imagining circumstances, and pretending conditions are *real* even if they aren't—or aren't *yet*.

And who's to say they aren't? No one can tell you that your make-believe doesn't exist because it's MAKE-BELIEVE. You are making it up as you go along. No one can deny your imagination! It's yours to own and to spin and to conjure and to create and to dwell within.

And that belief is the vehicle for your make-believe world to manifest as "reality." Because what is reality but another form of collective make-believe? We are dreamers dreaming a collective dream of what we believe our reality is made of. What a dollar is worth. What a house is worth. What an education is worth. What a life is worth. What "relationship" means. What's important. What's healthy. What's wise. What's wealthy.

It's *all* make-believe. We believe it's real and so it is.

Well, I'm here to tell you that even as "real" life is make-believe, so is the reality of our dreams that we wish were true. The better we are at make-believe, the better our dreams will manifest. The quicker they will be ushered into existence. And the more powerful and alluring a playmate we'll make of ourselves in this life.

Make. Believe. The more convincing our world of make-believe, the more conformed *this* world will become to *ours*.

Make-believe is powerful play. The play of a child: present, unself-conscious, elaborate, nonjudgmental, real.

Children inhabit worlds they create through play. They immerse themselves in colorful fantasy and spin out elaborate imaginings all their own. Interestingly, these are the same tools to effectuate and speed manifestation in our direction.

The more fully realized our imagined reality, the more accurately and expediently the Universe can match it.

Truth Serum:
By summoning our inner child, we create our reality through play and imagination. If we believe it, we can create it.

An Exacting Standard of Playful Perfection

"What fun! How perfect!" Exactly. Those two concepts taste great together — like chocolate and peanut butter.

Isn't is perfectly fun when fun goes perfectly? What if that became our new standard for life? Like a child who derives as much amusement from the box as the toy inside it, who sees everything as ideal, who takes everything as an opportunity to play? No mistakes. No accidents. No misfortune.

We can adopt this new standard. An exacting standard that is precise, true, faithful and uncompromising. One that measures perfection playfully. It's *all* perfect *all* the time. And it's *all* play... whether we like it or not.

In the same way a story we engage with in the movies, on TV or on the page needs copious amounts of drama to grab us, to hold our interest, so too, do we need drama in our lives. We need conflict. We need things to strive for, to surmount, to transcend. These are the opposing forces of Nature: we push *on* life and life pushes *back* at us. Otherwise, we'd be bored, a strangely unique human emotion.

And what is boredom? The feeling that there is nothing to do when there is *plenty* to do. With an infinitude of possibilities to explore how could we possibly be bored? Do lions gets bored? Or gorillas? Humpback whales or butterflies? Is there a tedium to how they pass the time? Not a chance. So why do we, as human beings, experience boredom? Because we desire drama. We crave conflict. Because we need something to push us — up, out and forward. And we need something to push back against — friction, challenge, resistance. We take on trials that foster growth and test our mettle.

When life hands us seemingly insurmountable obstacles, it's good to remind ourselves that we asked for it. Even as existence hands us its challenges, it simultaneously holds the key to unlocking their solutions.

Like a kid who creates a dramatic storyline to accompany her play, we spin ourselves dramas to keep life interesting and engaging. Like the child who sees the tree house, the sand box, balloons, blocks or a mud puddle as perfect and equal opportunities for fun, so, too, can we strive to view a universe of playful potentiality in all of life's circumstances.

Like the child, we may not get the toy we were expecting, but we get what we get and we don't get upset... when we embrace *an exacting standard of playful perfection.*

Then we'll find perfection in all things. We'll find ways to laugh and giggle and invent and create and elaborate and romp and stomp and rescue and vanquish and roll around in the mud, skin our knees, bump our funny bone, cry, laugh, twist, shout. All of life will become playful rapture... until Mom calls us to dinner.

Truth Serum:
We get what we get and we don't get upset when we
embrace an exacting standard of playful perfection.

Why Ask Why?

Sometimes *"why"* is the wrong question. Or the wrong question for right now. *Why* doesn't get you there. *Why* isn't really the question to the answer you seek. If what you seek is seeking you (as Rumi wrote) then *"why"* begs the answer "because." I am This. You are That. And That is all there is.

Why is a bottomless pit. A black hole. An abyss so deep no answer is sufficient to fill it. Because the answer transcends what will satisfy the human mind. By design. It's a thirst that cannot be quenched. For what would happen should you slake it? Satisfaction? Momentary. Because the Universe continues to expand.

The ultimate answer is that the Universe desires to know itself. It's that simple. Satisfied? Now you can go home. Game over. Sleep peacefully. But I've got a feeling that won't do it for you. You'll still have that itch. And in the morning you'll be scratching it, telling yourself you had the strangest dream about the answer everyone is seeking. The keys to the universe were yours. And then God, the Creator, the Beloved, the Divine, took them back. Leaving you scratching that itchy body part as you sip your morning cup of joe.

Why? Why? Why? Like a child's query — the answer always takes us deeper.

Why is the sky blue?

Because air molecules scatter light from the sun and blue light is scattered more than any other color.

Why?

Because blue light waves are shorter and smaller than other colors in the visible light spectrum.

Why?

Because each color in the visible spectrum has its own wavelength and amplitude.

But why?

Because our eyes perceive these waves as colors and color is one way we experience the world around us.

But why?

Because... because... because I said so!

Why?

Do you see? You can ride the plumb line of *why* down an infinite well—indeed you will with that inquisitive child—to return with a thirst-quenching bucket of water only to drop in again as you find your thirst anew.

And that's what we're here for: to augment the Universe with our own consciousness. Because we are all connected to it. The Universe's ambition to *query* itself is an effort to *know* itself in order to *expand* itself. That inquiry is furthered and enhanced by our questing.

"*Why*" is the rocket fuel for the journey of human exploration. "*Why*" is the reason we are here. And why not? We are created in God's image. We are not separate and apart from the Universe that birthed us into existence. We are part of one universal mind. We are aspects of a collective effort, set on a course of contemplating, investigating and unraveling. Through our seeking we unpeel another layer of experience. We become wiser. But we can never know it all.

But... why? Why? Why?

Just because.

Love the mystery. The Universe does.

It also loves you, Columbo, with your "just one more question." It also loves you.

Truth Serum:
The most important thing "why" teaches us
is to learn to love the mystery.

| MATTER |

Matter is immaterial.

~ Truth

What's the Matter?

The reason we are caught up in the material world, material things, possessions, "stuff," is because we want to MATTER.

We *need* to matter. It's essential to our existence. We are boundless, limitless spirits experiencing the material plane. And we've forgotten our divine natures while on this magic carpet ride so we look to the material world—the world *of* matter—in order *to* matter.

We seek to acquire, to accumulate, to consume... because we presume that MORE matter will matter. That it will make US matter. But matter doesn't care what we make of it. The material world doesn't suffer our foolishness.

But we suffer.

In our pursuit of matters material, we strive, we stress, we compete, we compare. We gain and lose, rise and fall, wish and weep. Destined to learn the material quest is an empty one. Barren, devoid, bereft. Even though it all feels so real, so gainful, so... material.

The irony is that matter is *immaterial*. Matter doesn't matter. *You* matter. Spirit matters. But the rest... doesn't matter. It's all temporary, ephemeral, transient, a passing dream that feels tangible while dreaming, but then dissipates like a mist in the warm rays of the sun.

So what DOES matter? That's a question for you to ask of yourself. You don't even need to know the why of it — why something matters. Just that it does.

What MATTERS to you?

What matters is a clue to purpose. Because purpose matters. And here's why: Being on purpose is how *you* choose the things that matter. How *you* choose what's important. How *you* set your own priorities to make your own meaning. No one else can choose for you and call it *your* purpose.

Choosing what matters is how you make your life matter to others, to the world, to humanity's evolution, and to the most important element of the equation — YOU.

What's the matter? You are. You've got to matter to yourself. Or you can't and won't matter to anyone else.

And that's the fact of the matter.

Truth Serum:
Matter... doesn't matter. But <u>you</u> matter.

The Heart of the Matter

Our purpose is to matter.

That's what we want. What we need. Our desire to be loved means we really just want to matter — to feel that we matter — to someone in the world.

The trick, aye, the rub, is that we need to matter to *ourselves*. The rest of the matter, one could say, is immaterial.

When we're faced with not mattering to someone we love or to the people or to the organization or to the client, the industry, the team, the project or to the community that matters to *us*, it's painful. Crushing. Devastating. If for no other reason than to make us understand that we need to matter to ourselves. No matter what.

We won't matter as much to anyone else. Ever. And no one else can or will matter as much to us. We will be continually presented this lesson throughout our lives. Once we throw ourselves into the breach, commit ourselves to the lovers, family, children, people, projects, causes, creativity, communities that matter to us, we'll be tested with our own relevance, our own mattering to each of those things. And when that test arises, we'll be faced with questions of self-worth, self-esteem, self-trust. We'll question if what matters has changed. If what mattered to us still matters. So if we're rooted in mattering to ourselves—to know in our hearts what *really* matters—then we'll still matter.

And that's the heart of the matter.

This isn't selfishness. But it is about *self*. Being of value, feeling of value. One day we may wake up and realize that we don't matter to the things we thought we did. Even to our own family. And that can be heavy duty.

I... don't... matter? Wow.

Well, we're just illusion anyway. An illusion of perception. But the Dharma, the teaching, the lesson is that it's *all* illusion, it's *all* immaterial. None of it is relevant unless *you* are. None of it matters unless you do. To *you*.

The irony is that despite *wanting* to be loved as we all do, matters of love are immaterial. Temporary figments of our imagination. Because the only thing that can anoint us with self-worth is self. To know, to feel, to believe that one's own experience has value, that one's own perceptions, feelings and convictions matter most. We can't place our own worth or the worth of those convictions in the hands of another. External validation is just that: it's *outside* of oneself. And that's a path to disappointment and disillusion.

When we say something matters we feel a pull, a tug, a quiet conviction about something. "This matters to me," or perhaps, "*You* matter to me." More than saying it, we hopefully act on our conviction so that the person feels we mean it. We consider them, we have regard for them, we include them in our thoughts, in our plans, in our hearts.

When someone *doesn't* matter, they feel our lack of regard. And they may try to show us that they do. To prove they do. In vain. Because how can someone make themselves matter to another? They can't. Mattering is binary: you matter or you don't. Just as someone may feel *we* matter, but for how long? Maybe we do, maybe we don't. Maybe we will and maybe we won't.

Mattering to another is temporary. Mattering to another is out of our control. Because mattering is a feeling *within* another. How can we control something *within* another? How can we influence a feeling? We can try. We can manipulate. We can negotiate, cajole, threaten, bribe, but any effect will be fleeting.

Think about the hobbies, possessions, artifacts, people, ideals, stories, and subjects that mattered in your life when you were five years old. Think about what mattered ten years ago. Three years ago. Last year. What mattered has certainly changed. What mattered only matters because we believe that it does. Our belief makes it so.

Some things matter for a lifetime. Some things matter momentarily. Some moments are momentous. Some are of no consequence. What's meaningful matters. And that's why choosing a life of meaning is how we make meaning, how we become meaningful, how we matter to others because we do what matters to ourselves.

So the only thing we can aspire to, the only thing we can control, is mattering to *ourselves*. Mattering to another is in direct correlation to mattering to oneself. When we carry ourselves with intrinsic regard, when you matter to *you*, when I matter to *me*, then we'll matter to *them, she, he.*

There is no other path to mattering. How long can you sustain mattering to another if you don't matter to yourself? If you don't treat yourself like you matter then how can another know to treat you like you matter?

How to matter? Purpose. Purpose certainly matters therefore our matter is certainly purpose. And purpose makes us matter. To the most relevant person, the only person who truly matters, and then all else flows: inner strength, confidence, self-worth, energy, movement, joy, abundance. When we *don't* matter to ourselves (and feel we don't matter to others) then it all goes out the window.

If a deer, a redwood, an atom chose to no longer matter to itself, to no longer hold the belief in its own meaning, then how long would it last before withering away and dying or blinking out of existence?

Mattering to others is temporary (except maybe to our parents). Mattering to ourselves is forever. It's our challenge, our gauntlet, the mantle of existence.

Self-worth. Self-esteem. Self-care. Self-love. Make it matter. Believe it matters. Know it matters. Because it does. Make yourself matter. Like nothing else mattered.

Truth Serum:
Our purpose is to matter.
The trick is to matter to ourselves.

*   *   *

SMATTER
(A tiny poem, or love song to oneself.)

Just a smidge,
A smattering of mattering
Is all we want, is all we need.
But the only one who matters
Is you to me.
You see?

I want to matter to you.
Want to feel a part of your plan.
Not apart and separate
From any other man (or woman).

Because what's true for you
Is also true for me.
And the only one who matters
Is yours truly,
You see?

Detachment Assurance

Surely we can do better than another attachment. And yet another. And another still.

Most of our lives are geared toward consumption. Nearly everything we do—digitally and otherwise—is driven by advertising which exists for the sole purpose of selling us things. Things we don't need. Things we wouldn't even know to want if it weren't for advertising.

Hurry! While supplies last.

Hurry in, sale ends soon!

Hurry — one day only!

Buy one, get one free! More! Faster! Buy it again!

Now we can do it with a single click. What's the rush?

If you walk the street or drive a car or ride the bus, a bike or the subway, there are plenty of ways to advertise something to sell you. Usually that item is unhealthy and fattening. But it's mostly fattening the wallets of the corporations hawking their wares, the businesses selling ad space, and the companies producing the advertising.

They're all counting on one thing — you're attachment to *more things*. In fact, they're so dependent on it, reliant on it and assured you'll be, too, that most products now come with an option to buy insurance for your attachment. This means *more* money to fund your addiction so that you won't have to suffer a partial or complete loss of your latest device, dongle, mattress, armchair, or TV. Now your attachment to *it* and its attachment to *you* can be maintained without interruption. All will be returned in working order or replaced with the latest and greatest — since your attachment is obsolete by the time you get it home.

We are the only animal with attachments. Every other creature on the planet lives carefree. The only thing bird or beast, fish or fowl are attached to is the moment and staying alive. Evolved as we are, we have myriad accessories, appendages and fixations that we've determined are essential for our survival and well-being: clothes, cars, homes, smartphones, computers, jewelry, silverware, stereos, cameras, surfboards, skateboards, bicycles, tennis rackets, canoes, waterskis, blenders, mixing bowls, skillets, lawn ornaments, LED lighting and on and on.

We're more like vacuum cleaners than kindred creatures. Vacuum cleaners function with attachments. They have nozzles and hoses, brushes and extensions, appendages and add-ons. But it doesn't change the fact that they suck. Attachments just help them to suck more, to suck better, to suck more purposefully. Now a human being is not a vacuum cleaner, but we must decide if our latest attachment helps us suck more, suck less, or if it just makes us a sucker.

Next time you see an ad, recognize that it is hocking—with rare exception—*non*-essentials masked as essentials; luxuries disguised as necessities; extravagances disguised as goods. But there's little good to be found in them. And the good derived will be fleeting.

Realize the next time you are offered insurance for a new purchase that it's an add-on you will be serving in the guise of it serving you. You won't own the product, it will own *you*. You'll work for it, pay for it, and the company that produced it will be grafted into your life for as long as you're addicted. Because that's the nature of attachment. Even if it's bad for you, you can't let go.

What's the remedy? The best insurance you can purchase is the assurance of *non-attachment*. And it doesn't cost you a thing. Non-attachment ensures that you have what you need, which is not all that much: a roof over your head, air in your lungs, food on the table and some love in your world. Be assured you can walk away from it all. From anything and everything. At the end of your life, that's precisely what you *will* do: leave it all behind.

All of your lovely things, your property, your wardrobe, your wealth (or your poverty), your friends, your family, the shirt on your back, the skin on your body and, yes, even what you now think of as "you." The whole shebang: this mortal coil. And if your *body* isn't you, then all of your attachments are even less so. They are not your essence, they are not your being, nor your reason *for* being. And anything that is not your essence is, by definition, non-*essential*.

Non-essentials get insured, but your essential being doesn't require it. It already comes with universal life assurance in case you're lost or damaged. Chances are, you *will* be lost and damaged many times over in your life. If you're doing it right. Being human, that is. But lost or damaged doesn't lessen you, doesn't mean you need replacement, doesn't mean you should be swapped out for the latest model.

But, hey, the multi-billion dollar insurance companies are betting on the power of attachment. And so far, they're right. They're playing the game. Preying on fear. But they can't get your essence unless you let them. So dial in what's essential. Play at being detached. Don't let advertising's attractive accessories hook you. Unless you absolutely, without-a-doubt, really just have to have it.

Click here to buy the audio book. Hurry!

Seriously, though, the audio book *is* available for purchase. Insurance is extra.

Truth Serum:
The only real insurance for your attachments
is the assurance of non-attachment.

181

GARDEN-VARIETY INSPIRATION

It's not a peak if you peeked.

~ Truth

Flap, Flap, Glide: From Fodder to Flight

The butterfly doesn't work so hard. Observe one. Its flight pattern is "flap, flap, glide." Flap, flap... then glide. A couple of short bursts of work, then it just lets things... slide.

The butterfly is pretty much blissed out (blessed out) all day long, every day of its life. And why? Because where it was once a meal for birds it can now soar *like* a bird. So the butterfly flap-flap-glides around, laughing at its luck, reveling in its good fortune, celebrating its success.

It lofts from bloom to bloom lingering in the fragrance of flowers. Once an earthbound, leaf-bound, creepy-crawly with limited locomotion it now floats with grace and ease from a grand perspective. As a caterpillar it fed on leaves; as a butterfly it feasts on sweet floral nectar. Being a caterpillar is a small price to pay for what's coming.

Is what's in store for you worth the price you are currently paying? Looking back from where you are now, were the dues paid for getting here worth it? For the butterfly, they seem to be. And even whilst a caterpillar, it wasn't thinking about paying dues. It was just being itself. The only being it knew to be. It's as surprised as anyone that it transformed into a butterfly. Who could've possibly imagined that?

Well, the caterpillar could. At the deepest levels of its genetic memory and evolutionary longing, the caterpillar *imagined* itself a butterfly. *Imaginal* cells catalyzed its metamorphosis from flightless to flighted. From furry and inch-wormy to fluttery and fun.

How can we be more like the butterfly?

Human beings have consciousness. And the power of imagination. If the caterpillar can do it, so can we: *We can become what we imagine.* Our own imaginal cells are vibrant and alive within us. As we activate them through imagination we catalyze the harmonics of the universe to transform us. We don't have to enter a chrysalis. The world around us *is* our chrysalis. We just don't recognize it as such. But we can harness its magic to evolve, to transform, to soar to the loftiest heights.

A friend once joked that butterflies are high all the time (as if on cannabis). They cluster together, hanging out on flowering plants. Sometimes one flops to the ground unable to get up. Why did he fall? Because he's stoned. And none of the other butterflies can help because they're flapping their wings in laughter at Ralph who is too far gone to cling to his own perch. Ralph flits on the ground unable to right himself. Intoxicated on life. On creation. On his own miraculous fate: "I was once a caterpillar!" His fellow butterflies applaud the proclamation, inebriated by their own splendid luck.

The butterfly is an inspiration for what we can achieve. We can go from babe to sage. From rags to riches. From fodder to flight. Aloft on diaphanous wings, intoxicated by fragrant flora, soaring beyond our humble beginnings, high in the air, high on life, fluttering with a gentle, mystical... Flap, flap, glide. Flap, flap, glide. Flap, flap, glide.

Truth Serum:
If the caterpillar can do it, so can we
become what we imagine.

The Sparrow's Dilemma

The sparrow, when it sees its own reflection in a window or sliding glass door, thinks it sees another bird encroaching on its territory and chases after it to discover too late that it's seeing its *own* reflection. The sparrow might head full-bore into the glass and knock itself out — or worse.

Similarly, when we meet someone who reflects who we are at our best (or at our worst), we can sometimes head directly at them with abandon, whether in love or in business or in our social or political circles and find that we're up against ourselves, battling our own best (or worst) qualities.

When we see something we recognize, we are projecting ourselves on the world and the world is reflecting that back to us. Sometimes that sets us on a course of going right after something as we are most attracted to the qualities in others that we possess ourselves — even as we are repelled by the aspects we don't like, which are also aspects of ourselves.

Like the sparrow, we go for it. Headlong. Sometimes the effort dazes us, knocks the wind out of us, renders us unconscious. It can even clobber the life from our bodies. We fling ourselves at reflections that resonate when the only resonance we are left with is the ringing in our ears.

A moment's pause might allow us to discern what it is we're driving so hard at *before* we dive in. Is it our own reflection in another? Attraction? Repulsion? Is it someone impinging on our territory? Encroaching on our domain? That's what drives the sparrow. Is it what motivates you?

Look before you leap. Or perhaps just look CLOSER before you fly headlong into something that won't yield, doesn't budge, nor give way to anything but a headache.

If it's too late and the world is spinning in the aftermath, ask yourself if the pursuit was worth the penalty. *There's a bulletin in the bruise.* And it doesn't mean you should chase the next injured bird that flits across your path.

Determine not to fly errantly. Allow the wee sparrow to teach its BIG lesson: Sometimes the thing you want to chase, or chase away, is *you.* An aspect of you. A reflection of you.

A vain attempt no matter how you perceive it.

Truth Serum:
We are most attracted to—and repelled by—the
qualities in others that we possess ourselves.

How a Seedling Became a Redwood

"Grow little seedling, grow! You can do it. You can do it!"

"Grow! Grow! Grow!" the other plants shouted.

And the seedling grew and grew into a giant redwood that protected and shaded all the other trees and plants and animals in the vicinity. And eventually raised a family of trees, and then a forest — teeming with life! Home to countless creatures, plants and bugs.

And the chorus of the redwood forest rose up to shout to the surrounding expanse: "Grow, grow, grow! You can do it!"

And the trees presided over the lands for a thousand years. And life flourished. All because one tiny seedling with the will to try was encouraged to grow. A minuscule, seemingly-insignificant seed had spawned a forest. It was an inspiration to all who gazed upon it. And inspired those who were brave enough, courageous enough, to encourage another.

Truth Serum:
A redwood seed doesn't think it's a seed.
It knows it's a redwood.

ALMOST HOME

Hope is the catalyst of courage.
Courage is the accelerant of possibility.

~ Truth

The Return

Returning to something you left isn't a slide back. It's not a descent. It's not a retreat. It's not giving in, giving up, nor surrender.

Returning to something or someone with a more informed sense of who and what you are is the definition of growth. The essence of becoming. Of evolving. Of being. Human.

The Return is really an *ascent*: it's climbing, progressing, scaling new heights. It's the part in the journey when the hero comes home having vanquished the dragon, defeated the tyrant, dispatched the warlord, rescued the princess, garnered the lesson and revisited the land from whence he or she came.

The Return is an essential—the *quintessential*—part of the journey that makes it mythical, heroic, complete.

The Return is what we will all face: A return to the womb. A return to Source. A return to the energetic potentiality from which we all arose. Our own life's journey is the apotheosis of return: we all die—a return to where we arose—with the wisdom and experience of a life, a battle, a romance, a learning well-lived.

"Live as if you were to die tomorrow, learn as if you will live forever" (as Gandhi advised). Because both are true.

Truth Serum:
Returning with a more informed sense of who and what you are is the definition of growth.

191

Alone, Together

Beyond all of the advice, precepts and guidance iterated in these pages, there is also the life path that the Universe has in store for you. Each of the seven and a half billion of us and counting is unique. Shaped by the experiences of our coming-of-age, our culture, our native land, our language, memories, birth place, parents, dreams, fears, feats, hopes, aspirations, goals, disappointments, lessons, perceptions, personalities, talents, challenges, circumstances, natures, health, looks, age, wisdom, soul-calling and so on.

There is a design and a plan beyond what we can perceive or understand. We're a part of it. We can be conscious co-creators of that plan. This is a call to action to trigger our awareness of and attunement to our greater role in Creation.

Each of us must walk our own life path. We all walk our paths alone, together. No two paths are alike. None have the same starting point nor arrival point. And there is no terminus. No ending. Just new beginnings. No fixity. Just transformation. No death. Rather renewal.

The collective will of our race, and of our planet, can and will be enhanced by our individual attunement to our role in the collective. By aligning with our purpose, attuning to our sense of success, we can fulfill our reason for being here and embody our role by sharing our gifts to enhance our own and everyone else's human experience. Remember that we aren't human beings having a spiritual experience, we are spiritual beings having a human one. Each of us has a life path. It's up to us to decide how to best traverse it.

As a yogi once urged, "Walk where your feet are." Keep your soles on the trail. Enjoy each rise and fall, each beautiful meandering. Don't rush to the end, don't fret about the destination. Allow the way's natural unfolding. Enjoy the splaying

of the road before you, attuned to its intersections. For perhaps one day our paths will cross.

Truth Serum:
There are no endings. Just new beginnings.

The Last Word

The last word on this subject is that there is no last word.

Even if you have the last word, it doesn't last. Life goes on. Your life. The other person's life. Seven and a half billion lives keep getting lived. And so any last word is just temporary, fleeting, ephemeral.

Getting in that last come-back or comment or slight or witticism or giving them a piece of your mind isn't really the last thing that will count, the decisive factor, the pièce de résistance, the final item that will tip the scales. The last word won't remain among the remains of the day. Because you could go on to greatness. They could go on to ignominy. Or you could go on to anonymity. And they could go on to celebrity. Or vice versa. Or none of the above.

In the final analysis, it will be factors *other* than words that really are the last word. And, really, there is no final analysis. Like the (Taoist) fable of the farmer with a solitary mare that ran away, which at first was seen as misfortune until it returned with a herd of wild horses that the farmer then wrangled, the ultimate blessing or curse of any life event should be met with "We'll see…"

As life turns and doubles-back, what was positive is now negative, what seemed like good fortune now yields misery, what appeared as compromise now feels like gain, what felt like waving the white flag now feels like victory.

So the last word is anything but. It matters not. No one remembers the last word or who had it — nor most of the words that came before or after. Might as well let the other person have the last word.

Words are cheap. Free, actually. It's our actions that express our priorities, as Gandhi recognized. Actions are the pictures of our lives; pictures worth a *thousand* words, worth *all* the words, worth *more* than words. How we live says it all. Which is why our lives are our message.

So to heck with the last word. In a word, fuhgeddaboudit (forget about it). Because the last word certainly isn't. The last word isn't what lasts. Only one thing is everlasting, which is why the last word is...

Love.

ABOUT THE AUTHOR

Truth W. Hawk is an author, artist and filmmaker combining creative entrepreneurship with spirit, people and purpose. Through his writing, films and global business leadership, he inspires and teaches fellow leaders, creatives and companies to empower themselves through a unique methodology of transformational practices.

Truth has taught branding and teamwork at Stanford and guided start-ups in media and technology. He's a veteran Hollywood entrepreneur who's spent more than 20 years discovering talent, shaping creative works and deal-making.

Truth resides in Big Sur and Amsterdam. He adventures around the world to capture stories of inspiration and meaning to share with global audiences. His mission is to spread the living principals of his work to catalyze individuals, organizations and thought leaders worldwide to succeed intentionally each and every day.

How To Succeed On Purpose is his first book.

Join the global adventure at
TruthOnPurpose.com